RECORDED VERSIONS
GUITAR ®

AUTHENTIC TRANSCRIPTIONS
WITH NOTES AND TABLATURE

Transcribed by
STEVE GORENBERG

Y0-ATJ-813

THE

KISS

GUITAR COLLECTION

PHOTOS BY JEFFREY MAYER

ISBN 0-7935-5973-1

HAL•LEONARD®
CORPORATION

7777 W. BLUEMOUND RD. P.O. BOX 13819 MILWAUKEE, WI 53213

Visit Hal Leonard Online at
www.halleonard.com

THE KISS
GUITAR COLLECTION

4
INTRODUCTION

7
ALL AMERICAN MAN

14
BETH

20
CRAZY CRAZY NIGHTS

27
DETROIT ROCK CITY

35
DO YOU LOVE ME

39
DOMINO

47
FOREVER

54
I WANT YOU

60
KING OF THE NIGHT TIME WORLD

66
LADIES ROOM

69
LARGER THAN LIFE

75
LET'S PUT THE X IN SEX

79
MAKIN' LOVE

84
NEW YORK GROOVE

90
NOTHING TO LOSE

94
ROCK BOTTOM

99
ROCKET RIDE

105
ROCKIN' IN THE U.S.A.

110
SHOCK ME

119
UNHOLY

126
GUITAR NOTATION LEGEND

INTRODUCTION
BY JYM FAHEY

When Kiss guitarist Paul Stanley was told, "You are bigger than The Beatles in Japan," he must have thought something like, "Yea, in whose dream?" Shortly after landing in Japan the group found it was true. more than 70,000 tickets had been sold for a series of 1977 shows at Budokan and all of those ticketholders and thousands more seemed to be waiting for Kiss at the airport. A decoy limousine fooled some of them, but the rest stormed the real limo and rocked it so hard that the shocks seemed about to give out. Kiss had finally arrived.

It wasn't always like that. Kiss formed in 1973 when bassist, Gene Simmons met Paul Stanley and they felt a comradeship. An ad in *Rolling Stone* led them to drummer Peter Criss, another kindred spirit. Simmons, Stanley and Criss advertised for a guitarist in *The Village Voice*. Soon afterward, they were sitting around their studio in downtown New York, discussing the guitarists they had already had seen, when a scruffy cat walked in off the street, guitar in tow, and without even a greeting, moved past them, plugged in and began to wail. The incredulous threesome decided to go with what was happening and once they began to play, Ace Frehley became an essential part of the band.

The band's name came to Paul Stanley while driving on the Long Island Expressway, perhaps not the ideal place for a revelation, but the Lord (of Band Names) works in mysterious ways. In any case, it was enough for Paul that the name was short and sweet and would look good in print. Besides, it was universal and covered everything from the first affection of puppy love to the kiss of death. Rumors that if referred to Keep It Simple Stupid or Knights in the Service of Satan have surfaced from time to time, but the group vehemently denies those stories, particularly the latter.

In the early '70s glam and "art" rock were king and androgynous fashion was the order of the day. It was not a huge step for a group growing on the scene, or even their fans for that matter, to begin wearing makeup. Kiss was not the first, but they certainly were among the wildest-looking. They would perform at rock clubs in full schtick and developed an aura of mystery around the band that really worked for them. They seemed to be seeking a look somewhere between Kabuki theater and superheroes on acid.

As time went on, Kiss left the rock clubs of New York and toured constantly. They especially loved the towns that were left off other band's itineraries. The contrast between the shocking look the band affected and the normal mid-'70s outfits of middle

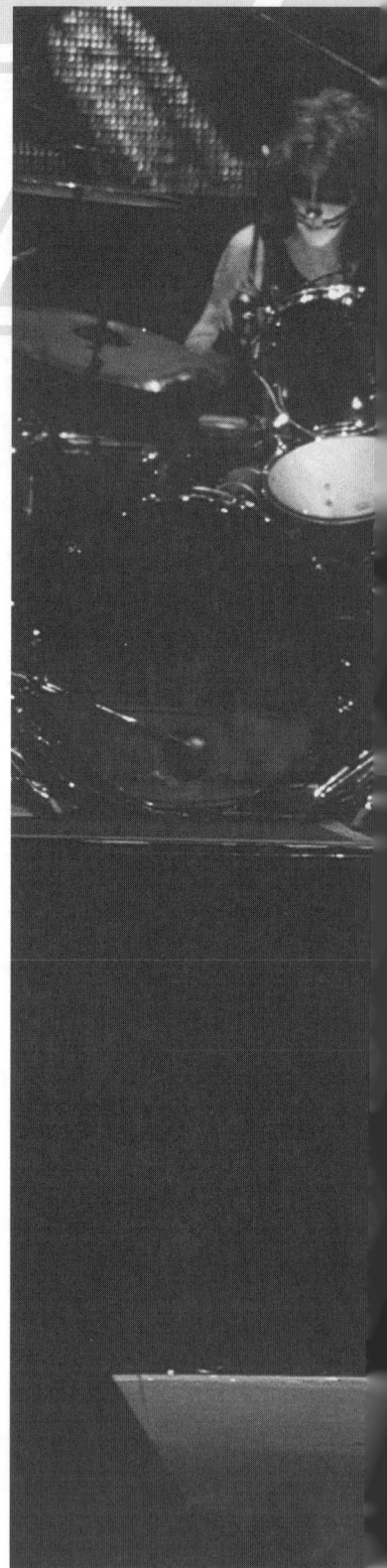

Photo by JEFFREY MAYER

America was remarkable, but their fans appreciated Kiss's attention to them. The flame-breathing, blood-spewing stage antics of Simmons won many more fans than they alienated and the Kiss "army" grew in number with every show.

From the beginning, Kiss believed their music was headed in the right direction, and it has continued moving that way. There has been a common element running through Kiss music in spite of their stylistic evolution. It's there in the braggadocio of the first album. It's there in the disco-flavored *Dynasty*. It can even be found in the thundering of their recent studio album, *Revenge*. The fact is, no matter what their image seems to portray, Kiss is at heart a pop band, in the best sense of the word. Both Paul and Gene will readily confess to their love of The Beatles, the undisputed champions of pop. Now, no one would accuse Kiss of being a Beatles clone, but the elements of melody and hook that made the *Fab Four* so great are deeply implanted in the music from the *Far Out Four*. As they have moved through their various stages (often punctuated by a live album), their devotion to the art of songwriting remains constant. That seems to be where critics have always missed the boat. By getting caught up in the trees of costuming, the forest of the music got lost.

While the critics dismissed the group as mere caricatures with none of the redemptive "artistic" content of say, David Bowie, the Kiss army of fans made up their own minds, and they bought over a quarter of a million copies of each of Kiss's first two albums, *Kiss* and *Hotter Than Hell*. Neither album had much in the way of radio play, and that trend has continued. *Dressed To Kill* came next and went gold, setting the stage for Kissmania which began with the release of *Alive*. Soon Kiss was headlining concerts for the very bands for whom they had previously opened.

By the end of 1976, the slings and arrows of the press could no longer hurt Kiss. They had become larger than life. In 1977 they became the first rock act to have their own comic book series. In it, the foursome battled the forces of evil just like other Marvel heroes, such as the Incredible Hulk and Spiderman. Of course Kiss could not be satisfied with being mere superheroes. They took it to the over-the-edge by adding vials of their own blood to the red ink used in the books (all supervised by professionals in the medical and journalistic fields). It was another hype coup by the kings of med'ia splash.

The mania didn't stop there. Lunchboxes, action dolls and in 1978 a feature-length, made-for-TV movie called *Kiss Meets the Phantom of the Park* kept the publicity wheels spinning, but those close to the band knew that it was spinning out of control. Peter Criss and Ace Frehley were altering their consciousness to unacceptable levels and each decided to go solo and leave the band behind. It didn't quite work out that way.

Instead Kiss kept puckering, replacing Criss with Eric Carr (who died in 1991) and Eric Singer. Frehley's successors were Vinnie Vincent (with whom the band became unmasked in 1983 on *Lick It Up*), Mark St. John, and finally, Bruce Kulick. The loss of their made-up image didn't seem to hurt the band's popularity. Kissmania may be a thing of the past, but their army has remained faithful and each of their albums from *Lick It Up* on has gone gold or platinum. In 1994 came the ultimate celebration of Kissness, *Kiss My Ass*, a tribute compilation of Kiss covers by a diverse selection of artists including Garth Brooks, Dinosaur Jr., The Mighty Mighty Bosstones and Lenny Kravitz.

Gene Simmons and Paul Stanley have the Kiss helm firmly in hand and seem to be ready to take the group into the next century unscathed by critical assessment or changing tastes. They also seemed to have mended any broken fences with Frehley and Criss, when the foursome appeared together for parts of MTV's *Kiss Unplugged* on Halloween night 1995. You can bet that Kiss will continue to do things the way they always have – their way, and anyone who doesn't like it can just Kiss off.♦

All American Man

Words and Music by Paul Stanley

A5

Tune Down 1/2 Step:
① = E♭ ④ = D♭
② = B♭ ⑤ = A♭
③ = G♭ ⑥ = E♭

Intro

Moderate Rock ♩ = 142

*A5

Gtr. 1 (dist.)

Rhy. Fig. 1

** Gtrs. 2 & 3 (dist.) *mf* P.S. (cont. in notation)

End Rhy. Fig. 1

let ring throughout

* Chord symbols reflect implied tonality.

** 2nd time only

Gtr. 1: w/ Rhy. Fig. 1

1.

2.

Riff A

8va

Gtr. 2

End Riff A

1. Ma-ma

full   full   full   full   full   full
20 20 (20) 17 20 (20) 20 (20) 17 19 (19) (19) 20 (20) 17 20

Riff A1

8va

Gtr. 3

End Riff A1

full   full   full   full   full   full
15 15 (15) 13 15 (15) 15 (15) 13 15 (15) (15) 15 (15) 13

Verse

Gtr. 1: w/ Rhy. Fig. 1, 3 3/4 times
Gtrs. 2 & 3 tacet

A5

told   me, _____   "Your la-dy's look-in' for an-oth-er man." _

_ I nev-er wor-ry, _____   there ain't a

need for me to take a stand. _____   I got my rea-sons,

the things I do are bet- ter left un- said. _____ I'm in- to

pleas- in'; _____ I do my talk- in' with my hands in- stead.

ⅅ.ⅅ. Chorus

'Cause I can make some time. _____ You got your tick- et and you're look- in' fine. _____

You're star- in' at the band. _ You want to land _ a

D **N.C.** **A5** **A5**

Gtr. 1: w/ Rhy. Fig. 1, 2 times

Gtr. 4

six - foot, hot look, all A - mer - i - can man. ___ Yeah. ___

Gtrs. 1 & 4

(Gtr. 4 cont. in slash)

Gtr. 4 tacet

Verse

Gtr. 1: w/ Rhy. Fig. 1, 1 3/4 times

A5

I've been to De - troit, I've been to

Gtr. 4

L. A. and I've seen St. Lou'. _____ I've had some good times,

but I've been wait - in' for a girl like you. _____ 'Cause I can

D.S. al Coda

Gtr. 1: w/ Rhy. Fill 1

1/2

9

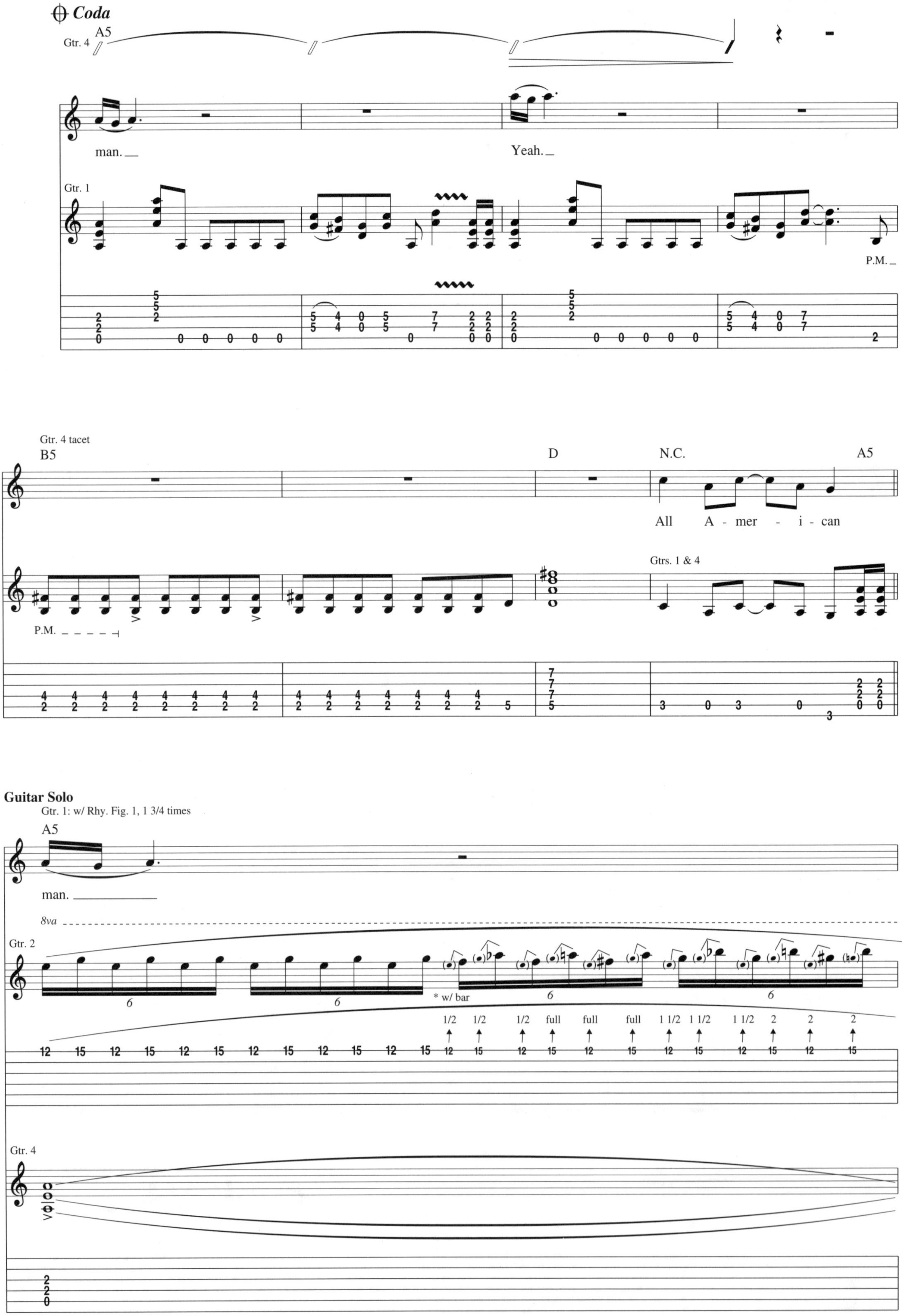

* Gradually raise and lower pitches w/ bar while trilling.

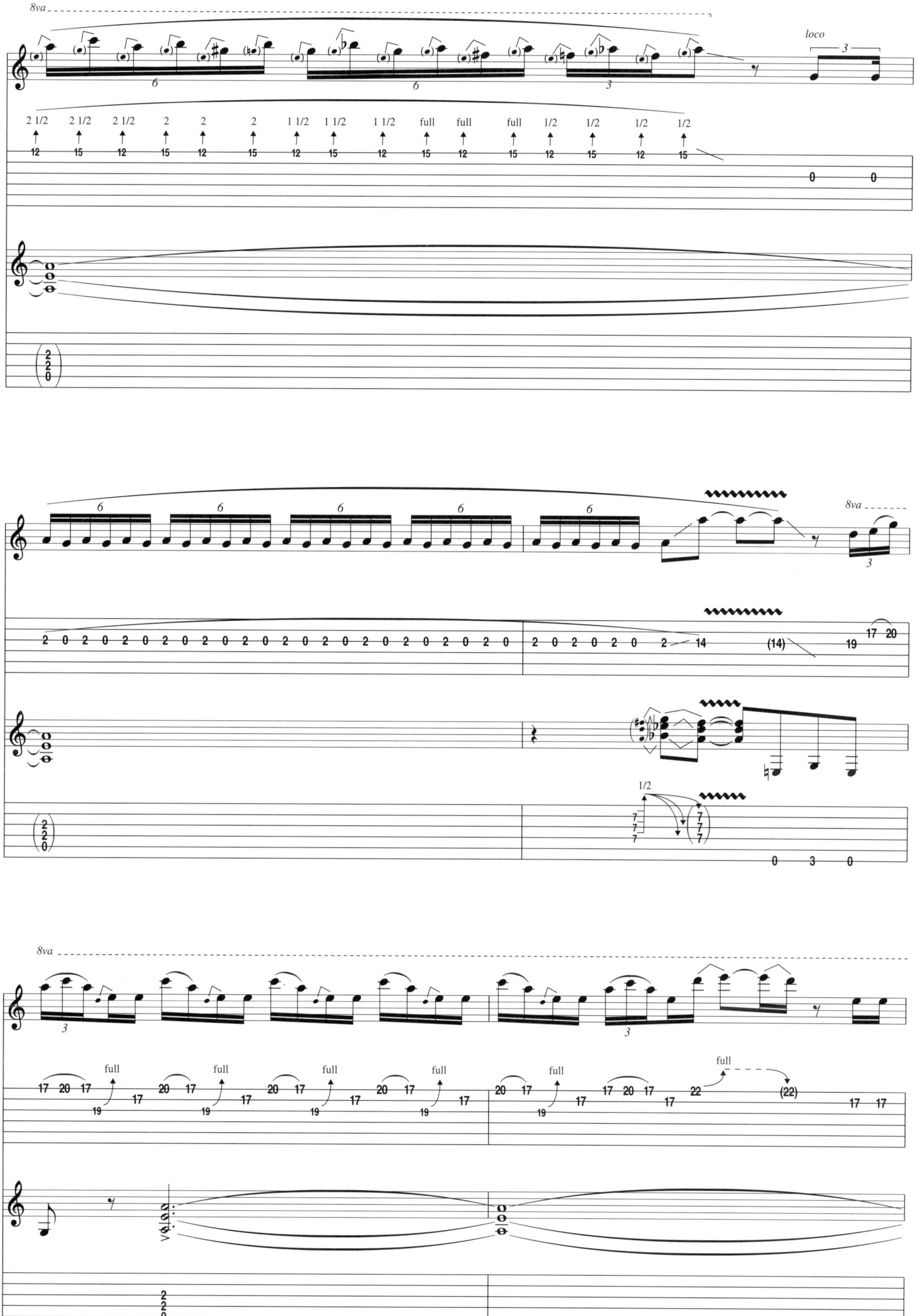
8va
loco
2 1/2
2
1 1/2
full
1/2
8va
1/2
8va
full

Gtr. 1: w/ Rhy. Fill 1
'Cause I can
8va
full
1/2
Chorus
Gtrs. 1 & 4: w/ Rhy. Figs. 2 & 2A
Gtr. 2 tacet
Em7
N.C.
make some time.
You got your tick - et and you're look - in' fine.
You're star - in' at the band.
You want to land
D5
D
Outro
Gtr. 1: w/ Rhy. Fig. 1, 1 3/4 times
Gtr. 2: w/ Riff A, 2 times
Gtr. 3: w/ Riff A1, 1 3/4 times
A5
a six - foot, hot look, all A - mer - i - can man.
A
Gtrs. 1 & 4
Gtr. 4
man.

Freely

Gtr. 2 tacet

I'm a six - foot, hot look all A-mer-i-can man. _____

fdbk.

Yeah. _____ Ow!

* composite arrangement

from *Unplugged*

Beth

Words and Music Peter Criss, S. Penridge and Bob Ezrin

Tune Down 1/2 Step:

①= Eb ④= Db

②= Bb ⑤= Ab

③= Gb ⑥= Eb

Intro

Moderately ♩ = 115

Gtr. 1 (acous.) **Rhy. Fig. 1**

*C   Dm7   G

mf

let ring throughout

Gtr. 2 (acous.) **Rhy. Fig. 1A**

mf

w/ fingers

let ring throughout

* Chord symbols reflect implied tonality.

C   Dm7   **End Rhy. Fig. 1** G

End Rhy. Fig. 1A

Verse

1. Beth, I hear _ you call - ing, but I can't come home right now. _
say you feel _ so emp - ty, that our house just ain't a home. _

simile on repeat

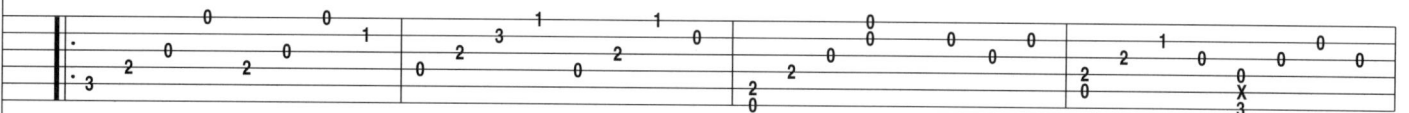

simile on repeat

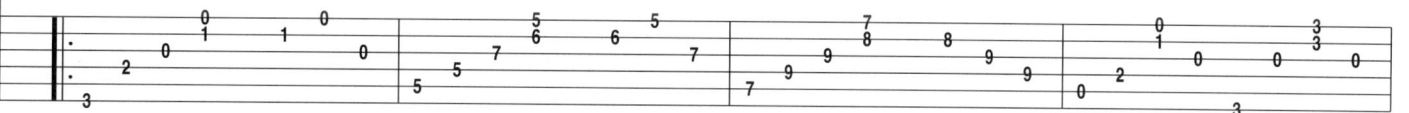

Me and the boys _ are play - ing, but we just can't find the sound. _
I'm al-ways some-where else, while you're al - ways there a - lone. _

Rhy. Fill 1   **End Rhy. Fill 1**

Rhy. Fill 1A   **End Rhy. Fill 1A**

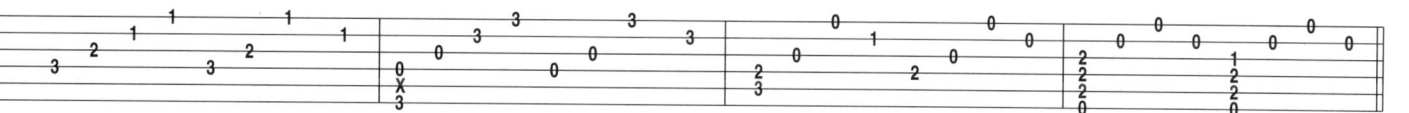

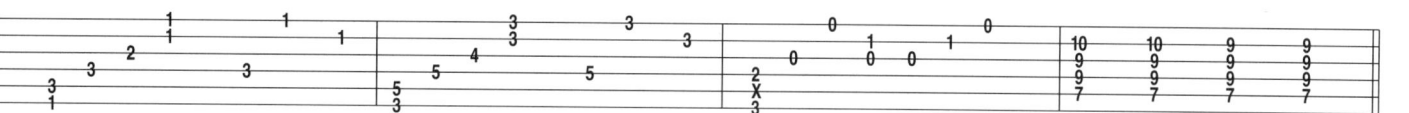

Chorus

Just a few _ more hours. _____ and I'll be right home to you. __ I

Rhy. Fig. 2

* Substitute F (① 1fr) 2nd time and when Rhy. Fig. 2 is recalled

think I hear them call - ing. Oh, Beth, what can _ I do?

Beth, what can ___ I do?   2. You   Beth, what can ___ I

End Rhy. Fig. 2

Interlude

Gtrs. 1 & 2: w/ Rhy. Figs. 1 & 1A   Gtrs. 1 & 2: w/ Rhy. Fills 1 & 1A

do?

Guitar Solo

Gtr. 1: w/ Rhy. Fig. 2

Verse
C
Dm
Em
3. Beth, I know you're lone - ly, and I hope you'll be al - right,
Gtr. 1
Gtr. 2
Am
G
F
G
'cause me and the boys will be play - ing all

Outro
C
Dm7
G
night.
Oo.
Gtr. 1
Gtr. 2
w/ fingers
C
Dm7
G
rit.
C
Spoken: All night
rit.
w/ fingers
rit.

Crazy Crazy Nights

Words and Music by Paul Stanley and Adam Mitchell

Csus2   Dsus2   Am7   Em7   D   Bm7
13411   13411   131111   13121   1333   131111

G   D/A   C/D   G^X   B♭   F/C
134211   132   1111   1333   134211   11333

Gm7   E♭sus2   Fsus2   E♭/F   C
13121   13411   13411   1111   1333

Intro
Moderate Rock ♩ = 122

G   Gsus4   G   D5   C5   N.C.   D   G   Gsus4   G   C5   G/B   D5   E5   D5   G

Woo!   *Spoken: Here's a little song for everybody out there.*

* **Rhy. Fig. 1**
Gtrs. 1 & 2 (dist.)

End Rhy. Fig. 1

ƒ

* When Rhy. Fig. 1 is recalled, 1st chord is tied from previous measure, not struck.

Verse
Gtrs. 1 & 2: w/ Rhy. Fig. 1, 1 3/4 times

Gsus4   G   D5   C5   N.C.   D   G   Gsus4   G   C5   G/B   D5   E5   D5   G

1. Peo - ple try   to   take   my   soul   a - way, ___
2. Some - times days   are   so   hard   to   sur - vive! ___   Oh ___ yeah.

Gsus4   G   D5   C5   N.C.   D   G   Gsus4   G   C5

but   I   don't   hear   the   rap   that   they   all   say. ___
A   mil - lion   ways   to   bur   y   you   a - live. ___

Pre-Chorus
Gtrs. 1 & 2: w/ Rhy. Fill 1
G/B N.C. D5 N.C. Csus2 Csus2 Dsus2 Am7
Rhy. Fig. 2
Gtrs. 1 & 2
They try to tell us we don't be - long.
Hey! The sun goes down like a bad bad dream. You're
Gtr. 3 (clean)
Rhy. Fig. 2A
mf
let ring throughout
Em7 D Am7 Bm7
That's al - right, we're mil - lions strong. This is my mu - sic,
wound up tight, got - ta let off steam. They say they can break you a -
Csus2 Em7 D G
End Rhy. Fig. 2
it makes me proud. These are my peo - ple, and this is my crowd.
gain and a - gain. If life is a ra - di - o, turn up to ten.
These are cra -
End Rhy. Fig. 2A
(cont. in slash)
Rhy. Fill 1
Gtrs. 1 & 2
(cont. in slash)
TAB

Chorus
G D/A Em7 Csus2 Dsus2 C/D Dsus2 G
Rhy. Fig. 3
End Rhy. Fig. 3
Gtrs. 1, 2 &3
- zy, cra - zy, cra - zy, cra - zy nights. These are cra -
D/A Em7 Csus2 Dsus2 C/D Dsus2 Csus2 * G^X
1.
- zy, cra - zy, cra - zy, cra - zy nights.
* Gtrs. 1 & 2 only.
2.
C/D Dsus2 B♭ F/C Gm7 E♭sus2 Fsus2
Chorus
Rhy. Fig. 4
Whoa. These are cra - zy, cra - zy, cra - zy, cra - zy nights.
E♭/F Fsus2 B♭ F/C Gm7 E♭sus2 Fsus2
End Rhy. Fig. 4
Come on! These are cra - zy, cra - zy, cra - zy, cra - zy nights.
Guitar Solo
Gtrs. 1, 2 & 3: w/ Rhy. Fig. 3, 1 3/4 times
E♭/F Fsus2 G G Dsus2/A Em7 Csus2 Dsus2
Yeah. Woo!
Gr. 4 (dist.)
f
w/ bar
-1 -1 -1 -1 -1 -1 -1 -1 -1
12 (12) (12) 15 (15) (15) (15) 15 (15) (15) (15) (15) (15) (15) X X
-4

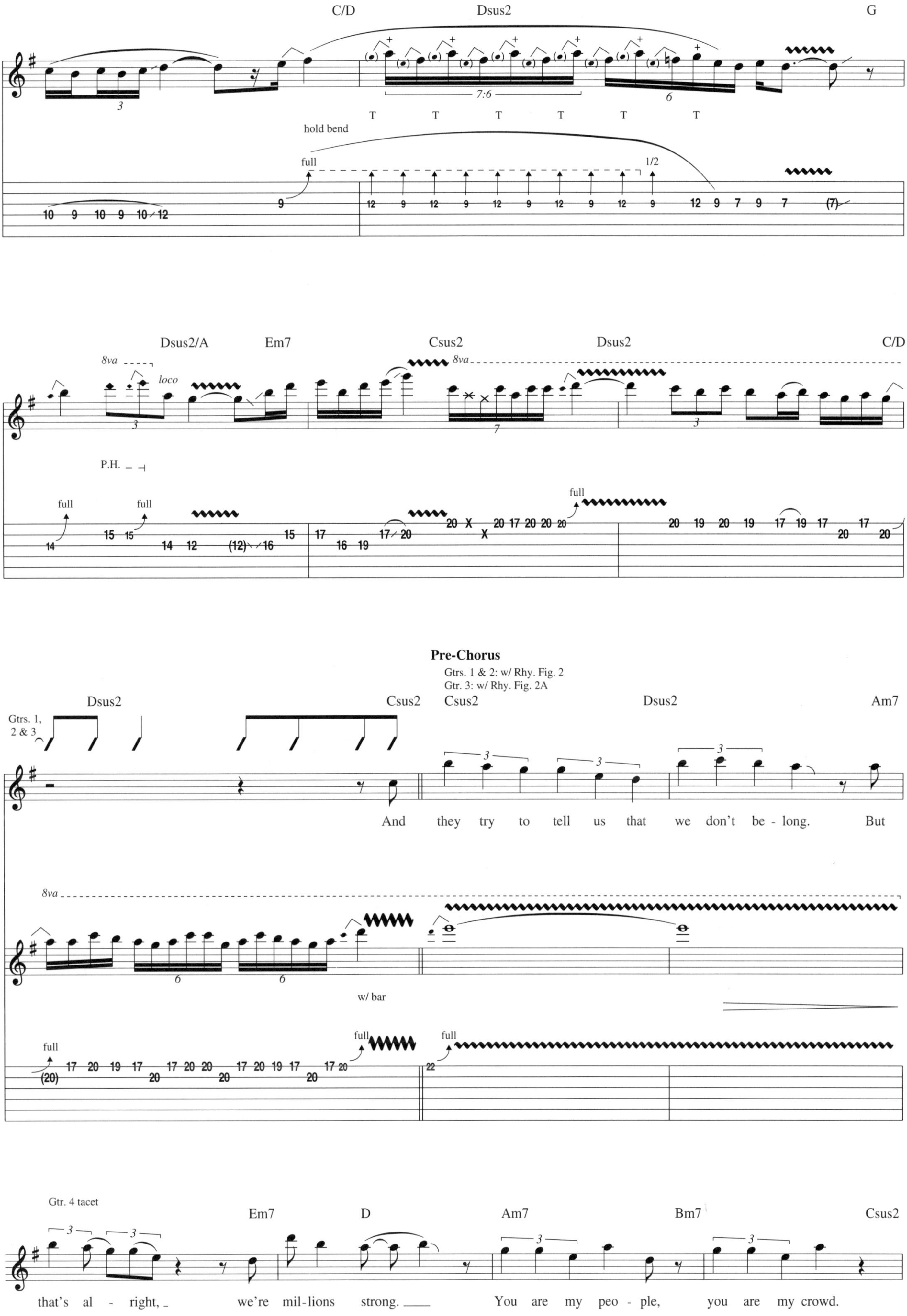
C/D
Dsus2
G
7:6
6
T T T T T T
hold bend
full
1/2
Dsus2/A
Em7
Csus2
Dsus2
C/D
8va
loco
P.H.
full
Pre-Chorus
Gtrs. 1 & 2: w/ Rhy. Fig. 2
Gtr. 3: w/ Rhy. Fig. 2A
Gtrs. 1, 2 & 3
Dsus2
Csus2
Csus2
Dsus2
Am7
And they try to tell us that we don't be - long. But
8va
w/ bar
full
Gtr. 4 tacet
Em7
D
Am7
Bm7
Csus2
that's al - right, we're mil - lions strong. You are my peo - ple, you are my crowd.

Gtr. 3: w/ Rhy. Fill 2

D   C   G

This is our mu - sic, we love it loud! ____

Breakdown

Gtrs. 1 & 2: w/ Rhy. Fig. 1
Gtr. 3 tacet

| G | Gsus4 | G | | D5 | C5 | N.C. | | D | G | | Gsus4 | G | | C5 | | G/B | | D5 | E5 | D5 | G | Gsus4 | G | | C5 |

Gtrs. 1 & 2: w/ Rhy. Fill 3

Spoken: Yeah.   *And nobody's gonna change me,*   *'cause that's who I am.*

Chorus

Gtrs. 1, 2 & 3: w/ Rhy. Fig. 3, 3 3/4 times

G   G   D/A   Em7   Csus2   Dsus2   C/D

Gtr. 3

Uh! These are cra - zy, cra - zy, cra - zy, cra - zy nights. __ Whoa, __ yeah._

Dsus2   G   D/A   Em7   Csus2   Dsus2   C/D

__ These are cra - zy, cra - zy, cra - zy, cra - zy nights. __ Whoa, ___

Rhy. Fill 2
Gtr. 3

```
    4
  # 4
T        3   3   3        7  7 7 7 7 7 7 7 7 7 7    7 7 7 7 7 7 5
A      5   5              7  7 7 7 7 7 7 7 7 7 7    7 7 7 7 7 5
B    5                    7  7 7 7 7 7 7 7 7 7 7    7 7 7 7 7 5
                         5  5 5 5 5 5 5 5 5 5 5    5 5 5 5 5 3
```

Rhy. Fill 3
Gtrs. 1 & 2

```
    4
  # 4
                                                        3
T  (12) 13  12                              7  7  3
A  (12) 12  12           5        5         7  7  4
   (12) 12  12           5        5         7  7  5
B  (10) 10  10           3        2         5  5  5
                                                   3
```

24

Dsus2 G D/A Em7 Csus2 Dsus2
These are cra - zy, cra - zy, cra - zy, cra - zy nights.
Gtr. 4
w/ bar
slack
C/D Dsus2 G D/A Em7
Yeah, yeah. These are cra - zy, cra - zy, cra -
w/ bar
Csus2 Dsus2 C/D Dsus2 B♭
Gtr. 1, 2 & 3
- zy, cra - zy nights. Hey! These are cra -
w/ bar
Outro-Chorus
Gtrs. 1, 2 & 3: w/ Rhy. Fig. 4, till fade
B♭ F/C Gm7 E♭sus2 Fsus2 E♭/F
- zy, cra - zy, cra - zy, cra - zy nights. Whoa, yeah.
8va
w/ bar
w/ bar
1/2
slack
slack

These are cra - zy, cra - zy, cra - zy, cra - zy nights.

Come on! These are cra - zy, cra - zy, cra -

- zy cra - zy nights. These are cra -

- zy, cra - zy, cra - zy cra - zy nights.

26

from *Alive II*

Detroit Rock City

Words and Music by Paul Stanley and Bob Ezrin

Whoo! Hel-lo!

Sat-ur-day night.

ra-di-o's the on-ly light. I hear my song, it

pulls me through. It comes on strong,

tells me what I got to do. I got to... Ev-'ry-bod-y's gon-na

(Get up!

Rhy. Fill 2
Gtr. 1

steady gliss.

B5

move their feet. Ev - 'ry - bod - y's gon - na leave their seat. _____
Get down! _)

N.C.   **A5**

You got - ta lose your mind in De - troit Rock Cit - y.

(Get up! _

Gtr. 1

```
6 4 6 4 6 4 6 4   6 4 6 4 6 4 6 4   6 4 6 4 6 4 6 4   6 4 6 4 6 4       2
6 4 6 4 6 4 6 4   6 4 6 4 6 4 6 4   6 4 6 4 6 4 6 4   6 4 6 4 6 4       2
                                                                       0
```

Gtr. 2

```
4     4 2   2       4         4 2   4   2           2       2       2
                                                                   2
              4                          2 4     0               2 4     0
```

Gtrs. 1 & 2: w/ Rhy. Fig. 1

                                                              B5

_ Ev - 'ry - bod - y's gon - na move their feet. Ev - 'ry - bod - y's gon - na
Get down! _)

Verse

Gtrs. 1 & 2: w/ Rhy. Fig. 2

C#5   **E5**

leave their seat. _____ 2. Get - tin' late, _ I just can't wait.

                                                  B5   **F#5**

Ten o' - clock, _ you know I got - ta hit the road. _____

Gtrs. 1 & 2: w/ Rhy. Fig. 2, 1st 7 meas., simile

C#5   **E5**

First I drink, then I smoke. Start the car, ___

try to make the mid-night show. _____ Let's go!

(Get up! ___

Chorus

Gtrs. 1 & 2: w/ Rhy. Fills 2 & 2A

Gtrs. 1 & 2: w/ Rhy. Fig. 1

B5   F#5   A5

Ev - 'ry - bod - y's gon - na

B5

move their feet.

Get down! __)

Ev - 'ry - bod - y's gon - na leave their seat. _____

Interlude

C#
⑤
4 fr

Gtr. 1 tacet
N.C.

* Gtr. 1

Gtr. 2

* Play 1st time only.

1.

2.

D#5

Gtr. 1

Gtr. 2

C#5   F#5   E5   A5

Gtr. 1: w/ Rhy. Fill 1
Gtr. 2: w/ Rhy. Fig. 1, 1st 2 meas.
B5
Gtr. 2
Gtr. 1: w/ Rhy. Fig. 1, last 2 meas.
Verse
Gtrs. 1 & 2: w/ Rhy. Fig. 2
C♯5
* While sustaining chord, switch toggle switch in rhythm indicated.
3. Mov - in' fast, do - in'
nine - ty - five.
E5
I hit top speed,
B5
F♯5
Gtrs. 1 & 2: w/ Rhy. Fig. 2, 1st 7 meas.
C♯5
still mov - in' much too slow.
I feel so good,
E5
so a - live, I'm so a - live.
I hear my song
Chorus
Gtrs. 1 & 2: w/ Rhy. Fills 2 & 2A
Gtrs. 1 & 2: w/ Rhy. Fig. 1, 1st 3 meas.
B5
F♯5
A5
play - in' on the ra - di - o,
it goes...
(Get up!
Ev - 'ry - bod - y's gon - na
B5
Gtrs. 1 & 2
E
C♯5
⑥ open
Gtrs. 1 & 2 tacet
(drums)
3
move their feet.
Get down!)
Ev - 'ry - bod - y's gon - na leave their seat.
Guitar Solo
Gtr. 2
N.C.
N.C.

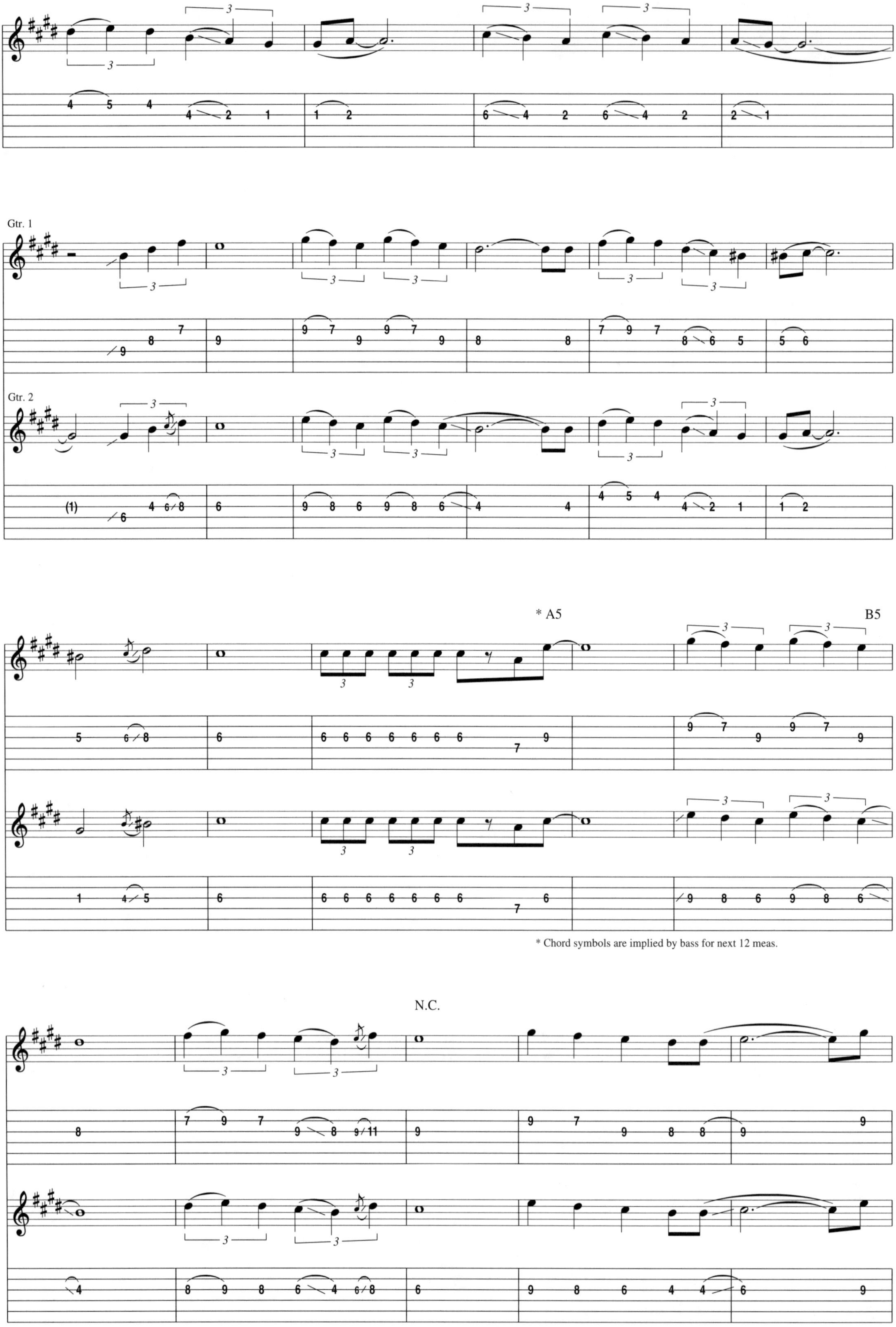

* Chord symbols are implied by bass for next 12 meas.

Verse

Gtr. 1: w/ Rhy. Fig. 2

C#5   E5

4. Twelve o'-clock, ___   I got-ta, got-ta rock. _____   There's a

Gtr. 2

Gtr. 2: w/ Rhy. Fig. 2, last 4 meas.

                                         B5   F#5

truck a-head, ___   lights star-in' at my eyes. _____

Gtrs. 1 & 2: w/ Rhy. Fig. 2, 1st 7 meas.

C#5   E5

Whoa, my God, ___ no time to turn. ___   I

Gtrs. 1 & 2: w/ Rhy. Fills 2 & 2A

                                 B5   F#5   A5

got to laugh, ___   I know I'm gon-na die. ___   Why?___

                                                          (Get up! _

Outro-Chorus

Ev - 'ry - bod - y's   gon - na   move their   feet. _____

Ev - 'ry - bod - y's   gon - na

(Get   up! ___)

leave their   seat. _____

(gong)

from *Destroyer*

Do You Love Me

Words and Music by Paul Stanley, Bob Ezrin and K. Fowley

A   E   D   F#5   B5   B5 IX

A5   A6   A5 type2   E5   F#5 IX   C#   F#

Tune Down 1/2 Step:
① = E♭   ④ = D♭
② = B♭   ⑤ = A♭
③ = G♭   ⑥ = E♭

Intro
Moderate Rock ♩ = 126

Verse

(drums) **3**

N.C.   N.C.

1. You real-ly like ___ my lim-ou-sine, ___ you like the way ___ the wheels roll..

___ You like my sev-en inch leath-er heels, ___ and go-in' to ___ all of the shows, ___

Chorus

A   E   A   E   A

Gtr. 1
(dist.)

Rhy. Fig. 1

mf

___ but do you love me? ___   Do you love me? ___   Ah.

Gtr. 2
(dist.)

Rhy. Fig. 1A

mf

```
T|----------------|--10------------|--10-----------|--10------|
A|--10------------|--9---9---------|--9---9--------|--9-------|
B|--9---9---------|--7---9---------|--7---9--------|--9-------|
 |--7-------------|------7---------|------7--------|--7-------|
```

D   A   E   F#5   B5

End Rhy. Fig. 1

(cont. in notation)

Do you love me, ___   real-ly love me? ___   2. You like the cred-

End Rhy. Fig. 1A

(cont. in slash)

```
T|----------------|--10-----------|--9-----------|--11----11--11--|
A|--7-------------|--9---9--------|--9---9-------|--11----9---9---|
B|--7-------------|--7---9--------|--7---9-------|--11------------|
 |--5-------------|---------------|--------------|--9-------------|
```

35

Verse
B5 IX
A5
A6 A5 A6 A5
B5 IX
Gtr. 2
- it cards, and pri-vate planes. Mon-ey can real-ly take you far. You like the ho -
Gtr. 1
Rhy. Fig. 2
A5type2
- tels and fan-cy clothes, and the sound of e-lec-tric gui-tars, but
End Rhy. Fig. 2
Chorus
Gtrs. 1 & 2: w/ Rhy. Figs. 1 & 1A
E
A
E
A
do you love me? Do you love me? Ah.
D
A
E
F♯5
B5
Do you love me? I mean like do ya real-ly love me? 3. You real-ly like

Verse
Gtr. 1: w/ Rhy. Fig. 2, simile
* B5
A5
B5
rock and roll, all of the fame and the mas-quer - ade. You like the con -
Gtr. 2
* Chord symbols reflect implied tonality.
A
- certs and stu - di - os, and all the mon - ey, hon - ey, that I make, but
Chorus
Gtrs. 1 & 2: w/ Rhy. Figs. 1 & 1A, 1st 7 meas.
E A E A D A E
do you love me? Do you love me? Do you love me, mm, real-ly love me?
Bridge
E5 F♯5 IX
N.C.(B)
Gtr. 2
(cont. in notation)
Gtr. 1
Gtr. 1
Gtr. 2
divisi
Your back-stage pass and black sun - glass - es

Outro-Chorus

Gtrs. 1 & 2: w/ Rhy. Figs. 1 & 1A, 1st 6 meas.
w/ Voc. Fig. 1, till fade
w/ voc. ad lib, till fade

Play 6 Times and Fade

Gtrs. 1 & 2: w/ Rhy. Figs. 1 & 1A, 1st 2 meas.

Voc. Fig. 1

from *Revenge*

Domino

Words and Music by Gene Simmons

A5

Intro
Moderate Rock ♩ = 138

N.C.

Spoken: Now, lemme tell ya my story.   I got a   man - sized predicament,

Gtr. 1 (clean)   **Rhy. Fig. 1**

mf w/ fingers

1/4   1/4

and it's a big one.   Goes   like   this,   yeah.

End Rhy. Fig. 1

1/4   1/4

Gtr. 1 tacet

D5   N.C.   A5   N.C.   D5   N.C. A5   F#5 G5 G#5 A5

My, _____ my.

Gtr. 4
(dist.)

3   *8va*   loco   3
3

f   P.H.
1/4

pitch: D

Gtrs. 2 & 3
(dist.)   **Rhy. Fig. 2**

End Rhy. Fig. 2

mf   P.M.
1/4   1/4   1/4   1/2   P.M.   P.M.   P.M.
1/4   1/4   *

* Gtr. 2 plays lowest note
of chords only.

Gtrs. 2 & 3: w/ Rhy. Fig. 2
N.C. D5 N.C. A5 N.C. D5 N.C. A5 F♯5 G5 G♯5 A5
Ow! Yeah.
Gtr. 4
8va
loco
hold bend
full
full
P.H.
Verse
Gtr. 4 tacet
N.C. A5 N.C.
1. Never had confession. Never had a home.
Gtrs. 2 & 3
Rhy. Fig. 3
End Rhy. Fig. 3
P.M.
1/4
1/2
D5 N.C. A5 N.C. A5 N.C. D5 N.C. A5 E5 N.C.
Never had no worry until I met Domino.
D5 N.C. A5 N.C. A5 N.C. D5 N.C. A5 N.C.
Ain't the Virgin Mary. Love her, I confess.
Rhy. Fig. 3A
End Rhy. Fig. 3A

Gtrs. 2 & 3: w/ Rhy. Fig. 3A
D5 N.C. A5 N.C. A5 N.C. D5 N.C. A5 N.C.
Got my hes - i - ta - tions 'cause she kis - ses like the kiss of death.
Pre-Chorus
G D A N.C. A5 G D A N.C. A5
Loves lots of mon - ey. Backs a - gainst the wall.
Gtrs. 2 & 3
Rhy. Fig. 4
End Rhy. Fig. 4
1/4 1/2
G D A N.C. A5 G D E
Calls me Sug - ar Dad - dy. She knows she's a - got me by the balls.
E5 E7 E5 E7
They call her Dom - i - no.
Gtr. 2
Rhy. Fig. 5
End Rhy. Fig. 5
P.M.
Gtr. 3
Rhy. Fig. 5A
End Rhy. Fig. 5A

Chorus
Gtrs. 2 & 3: w/ Rhy. Fig. 2, 1 3/4 times
Gtr. 4: w/ Fill 1
N.C. D5 N.C. A5 N.C. D5 N.C. A5 F#5 G5 G#5 A5 N.C. D5 N.C.
So fine.
Verse
Gtrs. 2 & 3 tacet
Gtrs. 2 & 3: w/ Rhy. Figs. 3 & 3A
A5 N.C. D5 N.C. A5 N.C. D5 N.C. A5 N.C. A5 N.C.
Ow. 2. Got a rep - u - ta - tion.
Gtrs. 2 & 3: w/ Rhy. Fig. 3A
D5 N.C. A5 N.C. D5 N.C. A5 N.C. A5 N.C.
Have - n't got a hope. It's a stick - y sit - u - a - tion if she ain't
Pre-Chorus
Gtrs. 2 & 3: w/ Rhy. Fig. 4, 3 times
D5 N.C. A5 N.C. G D A N.C. A5
old e - nough to vote. Loves to play with fire.
G D A N.C. A5 G D A N.C. A5
Loves to hurt so good. Loves to keep me burn - in', 'cause she's a
G D N.C. G D N.C. G D E
bad hab - it, bad hab - it, bad hab - it that's
Gtrs. 2 & 3
Rhy. Fill 1
End Rhy. Fill 1
Fill 1
Gtr. 4
8va
loco
P.H.
pitches: F# E

Chorus
Gtrs. 2 & 3: w/ Rhy. Figs. 5 & 5A
E5 E7 E5 E7
Gtrs. 2 & 3: w/ Rhy. Fig. 2, 2 times
N.C. D5 N.C. A5 N.C.
good, good, good.
They call her Dom-i - no.
Uh, Dom-i - no, Dom-i -
D5 N.C. A5 F#5 G5 G#5 A5 N.C. D5 N.C. A5 N.C. D5 N.C. A5 F#5 G5 G#5 A5
no.
Do it. Do it.
Gtr. 4
semi-harm.
1/2
Guitar Solo
* F#m
Gtr. 4
w/ bar
P.H.
P.H.
full
slack
Gtrs. 2 & 3
P.M.
* Chord symbol reflects implied tonality.
w/ bar
slack
Rhy. Fig. 6

Gtrs. 2 & 3: w/ Rhy. Fig. 6, 1 1/2 times
w/ bar
full
End Rhy. Fig. 6
P.M.
Gtr. 4
hold bend
1/2
* w/ bar
5:4
-2 1/2
* Dive bar while trilling.
Gtrs. 2 & 3: w/ Rhy. Fill 2
8va
N.C.
G5
loco
P.H.
semi harm.
pitches: E F# C# B A# D#
slack
Rhy. Fill 2
Gtrs. 2 & 3

Bridge

Gtr. 1: w/ Rhy. Fig. 1
Gtrs. 2, 3 & 4 tacet

N.C.

Spoken: Every damn time I walk through that door it's the same damn thing.

That bitch bends over and I forget my name. Ow.

Pre-Chorus

Gtrs. 2 & 3: w/ Rhy. Fig. 4, 7 times
Gtr. 1 tacet

G   D   A   N.C.   A5   G   D   A   N.C.   A5

Loves lots of mon - ey. _____ Back's a - gainst the wall. _____

Gtr. 4

15ma loco

P.H. _ _ _

full

pitch: E   A

G   D   A   N.C.   A5   G   D   A

Calls me Sug - ar Dad - dy. She knows she's a - got me by the balls._

3

N.C.   A5   G   D   A   N.C.   A5   G   D   A

_____ Ow! Loves to play with fire. _____ Love her, I con - fess. _

8va _ _ _

let ring _ _ _

full full full   full full full   full

45

Got no hes - i - ta - tions 'cause she's a bad hab - it, yeah,

Outro

bad hab - it, she's a bad hab - it.

Freely

Yeah.

* fdbk.

from *Hot in the Shade*

Forever

Words and Music by Paul Stanley and Michael Bolton

Cadd9   G   D   Em   C   Am   Am7   G/B   Csus2

Gtrs. 1-5; Tune Down 1/2 Step:

① = Eb   ④ = Db
② = Bb   ⑤ = Ab
③ = Gb   ⑥ = Eb

Gtr. 6; Drop D Tuning, Tune Down 1/2 Step:

① = Eb   ④ = Db
② = Bb   ⑤ = Ab
③ = Gb   ⑥ = Db

Verse

Moderately Slow ♩ = 88

*D5   Csus2   G   Dsus2   Cadd9

Gtr. 2 (elec.)   *mf* w/ dist.

Gtr. 1 (acous.)   *mf*

let ring throughout

I got-ta tell you what I'm feel-in' in - side. ___ I could lie to my-self, ___ but it's true. ___

* Chord symbols reflect implied tonality.

Gtr. 2 tacet

D5   Csus2   G   Dsus2

There's no de-ny-in' when I look in your ___ eyes. ___ Girl, I'm

Pre-Chorus

Cadd9   Am7   G/B

Gtr. 2   (cont. in notation)   Gtrs. 1 & 2

out of my head ___ o-ver you. ___   An' I lived so long be-liev-in' all love is blind, __ but ev-'ry-thing a - bout __ you __ is tell-in' me this time __ it's __ for -

(cont. in slash)

Chorus

ev - er. __ This time I know and there's no doubt in my mind. _ For - ev - er. __

* w/ Gtr. 5 on D.S.

To Coda 1

To Coda 2

Un - til my life is through, girl, I'll be lov - in' you for - ev - er. __

(Gtr. 1 cont. in notation)

Gtr. 3 (elec.)

mf
w/ dist.

Gtr. 1

Gtr. 3
divisi

Gtr. 4 (elec.)

mf
w/ dist.

48

Verse

2. I hear the ech-o of a prom-ise I made. When you're strong you can stand on your own.

But those words grow dis-tant as I look at your face. No, I

don't wan-na go it a-lone.

Pre-Chorus

An' I nev - er thought I'd lay my heart on the ___ line. ___ But

ev - 'ry - thing a - bout ___ you ___ is tell - in' me this time ___ it's ___ for -

D.S. al Coda 1

(cont. in slash)

⊕ Coda

Guitar Solo
Gtrs. 3, 4 & 5: tacet

ev - er. ___ Yeah! ___ Yeah! ___

Gtr. 6
(acous.)

ƒ let ring throughout

Gtrs. 1 & 2

* w/ echo

Em
D5
Cadd9
D5
Cadd9
8va
loco
8va
loco
Harm.
Harm.
G
D
Em
D
C
Whoa,
Gtr. 5
rake
Gtr. 6
divisi
*
* Gtr. 5 to right of slash in TAB
Pre-Chorus
Gtr. 6 tacet
Am7
G/B
C
D
Am7
G/B
I see my fu - ture when I look in your eyes, an' it took your love to make my
Gtrs. 1, 2 & 5

heart come a - live. ___   'Cause I lived my _ life be - liev - in' all ___ love is blind, _____ but

ev - 'ry-thing a - bout ___ you ___ is tell-in' me this time ___   it's ___ for -

D.S. al Coda 2

(cont. in slash)

⊕ *Coda 2*

Gtrs. 3 & 4 tacet

ev -   er. ___   Oh! _____   It's   for - ev - er, ___

this time I know and there's no doubt in my mind. _   For - ev -   er. ___

Un - til my life is through, girl, I'll be lov-in' you for - ev - - - er.

Yeah.

from *Rock and Roll Over*

I Want You

Words and Music by Paul Stanley

Chords: C D G5 A5 C5 G/B B5 F#5

Tune Down 1/2 Step:
① = Eb   ④ = Db
② = Bb   ⑤ = Ab
③ = Gb   ⑥ = Eb

Intro
Moderately ♩ = 102

*G   D   Em7   Cmaj7   D

In the morn-ing I raise ___ my head, ___ and I'm think-ing of days ___ gone by. ___

Rhy. Fig. 1
Gtr. 1 (12-str. acous.)
mf
let ring throughout

Rhy. Fig. 1A
Gtr. 2 (12-str. acous.)
mf
let ring throughout

* Chord symbols reflect implied tonality.

Em7   Cmaj7   D   Em7

And the thing I want out ___ of life ___ is...

End Rhy. Fig. 1

End Rhy. Fig. 1A

Gtrs. 1 & 2 tacet
C
D
Rhy. Fill 1
End Rhy. Fill 1
Gtr. 3 (elec.)
f w/ dist.
(cont. in notation)
I want
Chorus
N.C.
you.
(I want you. _)
I want
Gtr. 3
Rhy. Fig. 2
mf
P.M.
7:6
Gtr. 4 (elec.)
Rhy. Fig. 2A
mf w/ dist.
you.
(I want you. _)
End Rhy. Fig. 2
End Rhy. Fig. 2A

Verse

N.C.(G5)　　　　A5　　　　Em　　　Gtr. 4: w/ Fill 1

Gtrs. 3 & 4

Gtr. 3

P.M. ————————　　　P.M. ————————

1. You can run,　you can hide,　but you'll nev - er　get a - way.
2. You can walk　in　a haze,　you can trav - el　till you　die.

G5　　　　A5　　　　Em

You can lie　and de - ny,　but you know you're gon - na　pay. _____
You can live　in　a dream　and　your life will　pass　you　by. _

P.M. ————————　　　P.M. ————————　(cont. in slash)

G5　　　　A5　　　　C5　　　　G/B

Rhy. Fig. 3

Gtrs. 3 & 4

Nev - er loved,　nev - er thought you　could.　Treat you right,　girl, you know I　would.
Ev - 'ry day　that you hes - i - tate,　you're nev - er chang - ing the hands of　fate.

A5　　　　G5　　　　B5

End Rhy. Fig. 3

You can fight,　but to - night there's noth - ing you can　do.　I want

Fill 1
Gtr. 4

full　full　full　full

56

Chorus
Gtrs. 3 & 4: w/ Rhy. Figs. 2 & 2A
N.C.
you.
(I want you. _)
Ba-by, ba-by, babe, I want you.
(I want you. _)
1.
2.
Gtr. 3: w/ Rhy. Fig. 2, 2nd meas.
E5
G5
D5
Ah! ____
Guitar Solo
Gtrs. 3 & 4: w/ Rhy. Fig. 4
Em
D
Em
N.C.(A)
C
D
Gtr. 4
P.M.
Gtr. 5 (elec.)
f w/ dist.
full
8va
Gtr. 5 tacet
mf w/ dist.
f
Gtr. 6 (elec.)
Gtr. 4 divisi
Gtr. 6
loco
Rhy. Fig. 4
Gtrs. 3 & 4
1.,2.,3.
4.
TAB

* Echo causes note to sound into next meas.

Bridge

Gtrs. 1 & 2: w/ Rhy. Figs. 1 & 1A, simile
Gtr. 6 tacet
Gtrs. 3 & 4 tacet

In the morn-ing I raise ___ my head, ___ and I'm think-ing of days ___ gone by. ___

* Gtr. 1: w/ Rhy. Fill 1
Gtr. 2 tacet

___ And the thing I want out ___ of life ___ is...

* w/ phaser

I want

Outro-Chorus

* Gtrs. 3 & 4: w/ Rhy. Figs. 2 & 2A, 1st 3 meas.

N.C.

you.
(I want you.)
Ba - by, ba - by, babe, I want you.
(I want you.)

Gtr. 5

* phaser off

Gtrs. 3 & 4: w/ Rhy. Fill 2

Gtrs. 3 & 4: w/ Rhy. Figs. 2 & 2A, 1st 3 meas.

Ba - by, ba - by, babe, I want you.
(I want you.)
Ba - by, ba - by, babe, I want

Fill 2

End Fill 2

Gtr. 5: w/ Fill 2, till fade

Gtrs. 3 & 4: w/ Rhy. Fill 2

Gtrs. 3 & 4: w/ Rhy. Figs. 2 & 2A, 1st 2 meas., till fade

you.
(I want you.)
I want you.
(I want you.)
I want

1., 2.
3.

Fade Out

you. __
(I want you.)
I want
Ah. _____
(I want you.)

Rhy. Fill 2
Gtrs. 3 & 4

P.M.

from *Destroyer*

King of the Night Time World

Words and Music by Paul Stanley, Bob Ezrin, K. Fowley and M. Anthony

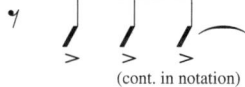

F5 C5 G5 D5 G5 D5 C♯5 C5
you're my head-light queen. I'm the king of the night time world,
End Rhy. Fig. 3
Verse
Gtr. 1: w/ Rhy. Fig. 2
F5 D G D G C G C
come live your se-cret dream. 2. It's so fine, lov-in' with ease, far from the house
Rhy. Fill 1
End Rhy. Fill 1
Rhy. Fig. 2A
Gtr. 2
* Played by Gtr. 1 only.
F C C5 F *C/E F C5 D5 D G D G
and the fam-i-ly fights. It's so fine be-in' with you;
End Rhy. Fig. 2A
* bass plays E
C G C F C C5 F *C/E *F/C *C/G D5
be-in' with me makes ev-'ry-thing al-right. I'm the king
* bass plays E, C & G

Gtrs. 1 & 2: w/ Rhy. Fig. 3, 2 times

D5   G5   D5 C#5 C5   F5   C5 G5 D5

__ of the night time world, __ and you're my head-light queen. __ I'm the king.

G5   D5 C#5 C5   F5   C5 G5 D5

__ of the night time world, __ come live your se-cret dream. Al-right.

Guitar Solo

Gtrs. 1 & 2: w/ Rhy. Fig. 1, 4 times

D5   C5 G5 D5   C5 G5 D5

Gtr. 3

let ring ____   let ring ____

C5 G5 D5

let ring   let ring ____

full

Gtrs. 1 & 2: w/ Rhy. Fig. 3

1.

C5 G5 D5   G5   D5 C#5 C5   F5   C5 G5 D5

Riff A1   End Riff A1

Gtr. 4

1/2   1/2   1/2

Riff A   End Riff A

Gtr. 3

1/2   full   full   full

2.
Verse
Gtr. 1: w/ Rhy. Fig. 2, 1st 7 meas.
Gtr. 2: w/ Rhy. Fig. 2A, 2 times
Gtr. 4 tacet
Gtr. 1: w/ Rhy. Fill 1
Gtr. 3 tacet
C5 G5 D G D G C G C
Gtr. 2
3. It's so sad, you're not con - tent; far from the mu -
8va
Gtr. 3
1/2 1/2 full
F C C5 F *C/E F C5 D5 D G D G
- sic and the ne - on glow. Ain't you glad we've got the time;
* bass plays E
Gtr. 1: w/ Rhy. Fill 2
C G C F C C5 F *C/E F C
far from our folks, they'll nev - er, ev - er know. I'm the king
* bass plays E
Outro-Chorus
D5 G5X C5 F5
Rhy. Fig. 4
End Rhy. Fig. 4
Gtr. 1
of the night time world, and you're my head-light queen. I'm the king
Gtr. 4
8va
Gtr. 3
divisi
full full 1/2 full full 1/2
Gtr. 2
Rhy. Fig. 4A
End Rhy. Fig. 4A
let ring throughout
Rhy. Fill 2
Gtr. 1
let ring
T
A
B

Gtrs. 1 & 2: w/ Rhy. Figs. 4 & 4A, 2 3/4 times
*D5 G5/D C5/D F5/D
of the night time world, come live your se - cret dream. I'm the king.
8va
Gtr. 4
Gtr. 3
divisi
full
full
1/2
full
full
1/2
* Chord symbols reflect combined tonality.
Gtr. 3: w/ Riff A, 2 times
Gtr. 4 tacet
D5 G5/D C5/D F5/D
I'm the king. I'm the king. I'm the king. I'm the king.
Gtr. 2: w/ Rhy. Fill 3
Gtr. 4: w/ Fill 2
D5 G5/D C5/D F5 C5 G5 D5
Gtr. 1
I'm the king. I'm the king. I'm the king. I'm the king.
Gtrs. 1 & 2: w/ Rhy. Fig. 3, 2 times
Gtrs. 3 & 4: w/ Riffs A & A1, 2 times
G5 D5 C♯5 C5 F5 C5 G5 D5
of the night time world, and you're my head-light queen. I'm the king
Play 3 Times and Fade
G5 D5 C♯5 C5 F5 C5 G5 D5
of the night time world, come live your se - cret dream. I'm the king.
Rhy. Fill 3
Gtr. 2
Fill 2
Gtr. 4

from *Rock and Roll Over*

Ladies Room

Words and Music by Gene Simmons

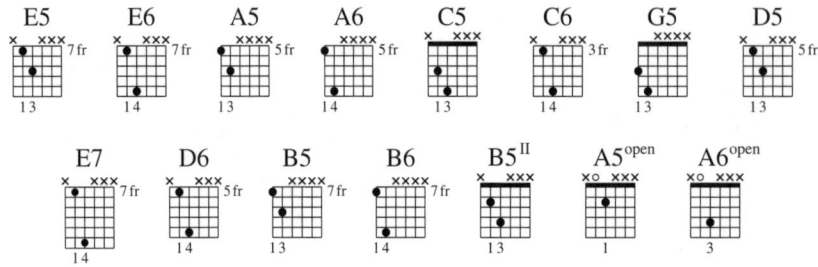

E5 E6 A5 A6 C5 C6 G5 D5

E7 D6 B5 B6 B5^{II} A5^{open} A6^{open}

Tune Down 1/2 Step:
① = Eb   ④ = Db
② = Bb   ⑤ = Ab
③ = Gb   ⑥ = Eb

Intro

Moderate Rock ♩ = 132

E5   E6 E5 E6 E5   A5   A6 A5 A6 A5   E5   E6 E5 E6 E5   A5   A6 A5 A6 A5   C5

Rhy. Fig. 1A

Gtr. 2 (dist.)   *mf*

Gtr. 1 (dist.)   Rhy. Fig. 1

mf let ring throughout

C6 C5 C6 C5   G5   D5   E5   E6 E5   E6 E5   E7 E5 E6 E5   D5

End Rhy. Fig. 1A

End Rhy. Fig. 1

(cont. in slash)

Verse

D5 D6 D5   A5   A6 A5   E5   E6 E5   B5   B6 B5   D5

Rhy. Fig. 2

Gtrs. 1 & 2

1. Ev-'ry time it's the same, __ what fol-lows me is my __ fame. __

D6 D5   A5   A6 A5   E5   E6 E5   E6 E5   E7 E5 E6 E5   D5

End Rhy. Fig. 2

You're what I need __ to play __ the game. __

Verse

*Gtrs. 1 & 2: w/ Rhy. Fig. 2

D5   D6 D5   A5   A6 A5   E5   E6 E5   B5   B6 B5   D5

2. You say you like to dance, _____   mm,   I think I'll take the chance. _____
3. You say you like to play, _____   well,   it's too late for you to get a - way. _

* 1st chord of Rhy. Fig. 2 is tied, not struck.

Gtr. 3: w/ Fill 1, 2nd time

D6 D5   A5   A6 A5   E5   E6 E5   E6 E5 E7 E5 E6 E5   B5 II C5

Rhy. Fill 1   End Rhy. Fill 1

Gtrs.
1 & 2

Oo ba - by,   may - be it's time for ro - mance. _____
And you've got - ta be - lieve ___ me   when I say. _____   Ba - by, now. _____

Pre-Chorus

Rhy. Fig. 3   D5   A5 open   A6 open A5 open   C5

You're such a jewel in the rough. _____   You wan - na show me your stuff. _____

C6 C5   D5   D6 D5   A5   End Rhy. Fig. 3

For my mon - ey   you can't be too soon. ___

Chorus

* Gtrs. 1 & 2: w/ Rhy. Figs. 1 & 1A, 1st time
* Gtrs. 1 & 2: w/ Rhy. Figs. 1 & 1A, 1st 6 meas., 2nd time

E5 E6 E5 E6 E5   A5   A6 A5 A6 A5 E5   E6 E5 E6 E5   A5   A6 A5 A6 A5 C5

Meet,   meat you in the la - dies room. _____   Meet,   meat you in the la - dies room. _____

* 1st note/chord of Rhy. Figs. 1 & 1A are struck, not tied.

1.

C6 C5 C6 C5   G5   D5   E5   E6 E5   E6 E5 E7 E5 E6 E5 D5

For my mon - ey   you can't be too soon. ___

Fill 1
Gtr. 3 (dist.)

f

```
T  12  12 12/12 12 12    12    12
A  12  12 12/12 12 12    12    12
B                        14 14 (14)
                         14 14 (14)
```

67

2.
Guitar Solo
Gtrs. 1 & 2: w/ Rhy. Figs. 1 & 1A, 1st 7 meas.
D5 E5 E6 E5 E6 E5 A5 A6 A5 A6 A5 E5 E6 E5 E6 E5 A5
you can't be too soon.
Gtr. 3
let ring
A6 A5 A6 A5 C5 C6 C5 C6 C5 G5 D5 E5 E6 E5 E6 E5
You can't be too soon.
let ring
full
Pre-Chorus
Gtrs. 1 & 2: w/ Rhy. Fig. 3
Gtr. 3 tacet
Gtrs. 1 & 2: w/ Rhy. Fill 1
E7 E5 E6 E5 B5 C5 D5 A5
You're such a jewel in the rough.
You wan-na show me your stuff.
full full
A6 A5 C5 C6 C5 D5 D6 D5 A5
Come on ba-by. For my mon-ey you can't be too soon.
Outro-Chorus
* Gtrs. 1 & 2: w/ Rhy. Figs. 1 & 1A, 1st 6 meas.
E5 E6 E5 E6 E5 A5 A6 A5 A6 A5 E5 E6 E5 E6 E5 A5 A6 A5 A6 A5 C5
Meet, meat you in the la-dies room. I'll meet you, greet you in the la-dies room.
* 1st note/chord of Rhy. Figs. 1 & 1A are struck, not tied.
Gtrs. 1 & 2: w/ Rhy. Figs. 1 & 1A, 1st 6 meas.
C6 C5 C6 C5 G5 D5 E5 E6 E5 E6 E5 A5 A6 A5 A6 A5 E5
For my mon-ey you can't be too soon. Meet you, greet you in the la-dies room. I'll
Play 4 Times and Fade
E6 E5 E6 E5 A5 A6 A5 A6 A5 C5 C6 C5 C6 C5 G5 D5 E5
meet you, greet you in the la-dies room. For my mon-ey you can't be too soon.

from *Alive II*

Larger than Life

Words and Music by Gene Simmons

Tune Down 1/2 Step:
① = E♭   ④ = D♭
② = B♭   ⑤ = A♭
③ = G♭   ⑥ = E♭

Intro

Moderately Slow Rock ♩ = 85

Gtr. 1 (dist.)

mf

1. Do you wan-na make be - lieve? _____

let ring

Verse

Gtr. 1: w/ Rhy. Fig. 1, 3 times

Gtr. 2 tacet

There's noth-in' up my sleeve.   I'm a man as man can be, _____ as you can plain - ly see.

Don't wan - na see ___ no tears, _____ al - le - vi - ate your ___ fears.

Gtr. 1: w/ Rhy. Fig. 2

When you think you've seen __ it all, _____ ba - by...

Pre-Chorus

You can't be - lieve __ your __ eyes, _____ what you heard were-n't lies. __

Gtr. 1   **Rhy. Fig. 3**

My love __ is too much to hold, __ too much to hold. _____

End Rhy. Fig. 3

Interlude

Gtr. 1: w/ Rhy. Fig. 2, 2 times

Uh!   M - much too much. _____

Verse

Gtr. 1: w/ Rhy. Fig. 1, 5 times

2. I'm some-one you __ can fight, _____ I'm pain in size. You can't __ be - lieve __ your eyes, _____

what you heard were not lies. I'm too much too hold, _____ I can't be bought or sold.

I'm far more than a man, _____ I'm gon-na make you __ un - der-stand. _____ I'm a-larg-er than __

Pre-Chorus
Gtr. 1: w/ Rhy. Fig. 2
Gtr. 1: w/ Rhy. Fig. 3
A G/A A G/A
A G/A A G/A G5/D D A G/A A G/A F C G D E D
life - size man.
And you can't be - lieve your eyes,
E D E D E D E
what you heard were-n't lies.
My love is too much to hold,
too much to hold.
Chorus
G D/A A D A D A G D/A
My love is larg-er than life, mm, larg - er than life.
My love is
Rhy. Fig. 4
Gtr. 1
A D A D A G D/A *Cadd9
larg-er than life, a - larg-er than life.
My love is too much to hold,
let ring
* Chord symbols reflect implied tonality.
Guitar Solo
Gtr. 1: w/ Rhy. Fig. 2, 4 times
G/B D A G/A A G/A G5/D D
it can't be sold. Whoa, no.
End Rhy. Fig. 4
8va
Gtr. 2
fdbk.
let ring
full

You can't be - lieve ___ your . eyes, ___

Pre-Chorus
Gtr. 1: w/ Rhy. Fig. 3

Gtr. 2 tacet

what you heard were-n't lies. ___ My love ___ is too much to hold, ___ too much to hold. _____

Chorus
Gtr. 1: w/ Rhy. Fig. 4
G D/A A D A D A G D/A
My love is larg-er than life, larg-er than life. My love is
A D A D A G D/A Cadd9
larg-er than life, larg - er than life. My love is too much to hold,
Interlude
Gtr. 1: w/ Rhy. Fig. 2, 4 times
G/B D A G/A A G/A G5/D D
it can't be sold. Whoa, no.
Gtr. 2
full
A G/A A G/A F C G D A G/A A G/A G5/DD A G/AA G/A F C G D
I'm a larg-er than life - size man.
8va loco
P.H.
full
full
1 1/2
pitch: B
Outro-Chorus
Gtr. 1: w/ Rhy. Fig. 4, 1st 5 meas.
Gtr. 2 tacet
G D/A A D A D A
My love is larg - er than life, larg - er than life.
G D/A A D A D A G D/A
My love is larg-er than life, mm, larg - er than life. My love is

Cadd9 D F G A5
too much to hold, it can't be sold. Whoa, no!
Gtr. 2
8va
let ring
full
Gtr. 1
let ring
Freely

from *Smashes, Thrashes & Hits*

Let's Put the X in Sex

Words and Music by Paul Stanley and Desmond Child

I knew her bod - y, but I could - n't see her face. She
asked her who was call - ing, but she was - n't play - ing fair. Some -

D
N.C.

Pre-Chorus

E5　E6　E5　E6　E5　E6　E5　F#5　G5

did - n't leave a num - ber, not an ad - dress or a clue, but
times you got - ta suf - fer for the pleas - ure that you seek. You're

Gtr. 1

Gtr. 2

D

some - thing in that pho - to - graph re - mind - ed me of you. Ba - by, let's ___
beg - gin' for an eye - ful, but you on - ly get a peek.

Rhy. Fill 1　End Rhy. Fill 1

w/ phaser

Rhy. Fill 1A　End Rhy. Fill 1A

w/ phaser

full

Chorus

Gtr. 1: w/ Rhy. Fig. 2, 1 1/2 times
Gtr. 2: w/ Riff A

A5　G5　D　N.C.

___ put the X in sex. ___ Love's like a mus - cle and you make me wan - na flex. Ba - by, let's___ put the X in sex. ___ Keep it un-der-cov-er, ba-by, let me be your pri-vate eye. ___

Keep it un-der-cov-er, ba-by, let me be your pri-vate eye. ___

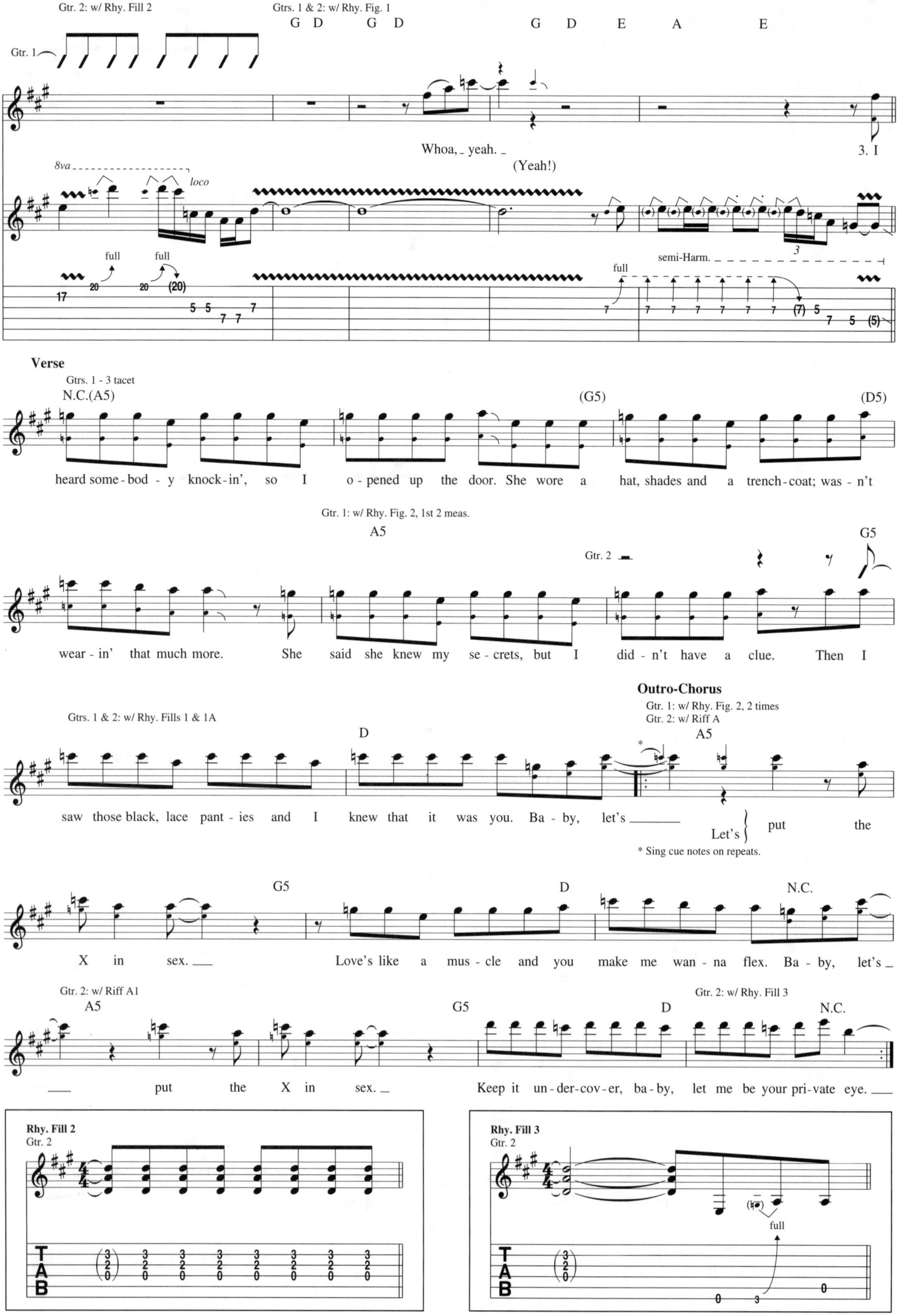

Gtr. 2: w/ Rhy. Fill 2
Gtrs. 1 & 2: w/ Rhy. Fig. 1
G D G D G D E A E
Gtr. 1
Whoa, yeah.
(Yeah!)
3. I
8va
loco
full
full
semi-Harm.
Verse
Gtrs. 1 - 3 tacet
N.C.(A5)
(G5)
(D5)
heard some-bod - y knock-in', so I o-pened up the door. She wore a hat, shades and a trench-coat; was - n't
Gtr. 1: w/ Rhy. Fig. 2, 1st 2 meas.
A5
G5
Gtr. 2
wear - in' that much more. She said she knew my se - crets, but I did - n't have a clue. Then I
Outro-Chorus
Gtrs. 1 & 2: w/ Rhy. Fills 1 & 1A
Gtr. 1: w/ Rhy. Fig. 2, 2 times
Gtr. 2: w/ Riff A
D
A5
saw those black, lace pant - ies and I knew that it was you. Ba - by, let's
Let's put the
* Sing cue notes on repeats.
G5
D
N.C.
X in sex. Love's like a mus - cle and you make me wan - na flex. Ba - by, let's
Gtr. 2: w/ Riff A1
Gtr. 2: w/ Rhy. Fill 3
A5
G5
D
N.C.
put the X in sex. Keep it un-der-cov-er, ba-by, let me be your pri-vate eye.
Rhy. Fill 2
Gtr. 2
Rhy. Fill 3
Gtr. 2
full

from *Rock and Roll Over*

Makin' Love

Words and Music by Paul Stanley and S. Delaney

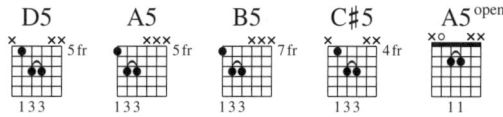

D5   A5   B5   C#5   A5 open

Intro
Moderately Fast Rock ♩ = 167

*E5

Rhy. Fig. 1

Gtr. 1 (elec.)

End Rhy. Fig. 1

mf w/ dist.   P.M.   P.M.   P.M.   P.M.   P.M.   P.M.   P.M.

P.M.

let ring

* Chord symbols reflect implied tonality.

Rhy. Fig. 1A

Gtr. 2 (elec.)

End Rhy. Fig. 1A

mf w/ dist.   P.M.   P.M.   P.M.   P.M.   P.M.

P.M.

Verse

Gtrs. 1 & 2: w/ Rhy. Fig. 1 & 1A, 1st 3 meas.

E5

D5   A5   B5

Gtrs. 1 & 2

1. I just hate ___ when the girl says wait! *(echo repeats)*   I real-ly want ___ her

Gtrs. 1 & 2: w/ Rhy. Figs. 1 & 1A, 1st 3 meas.

E5

D5   A5   B5

Gtrs. 1 & 2

by my side. Don't hes-i-tate. _____   I real-ly want ___ her

* Single echo repeat on the
word "love" throughout choruses.

Gtrs. 1 & 2: w/ Rhy. Figs. 3 & 3A, 1st 3 meas.

E5   D5   A5 open

_____ mak-in' love, _____ mak-in' love _____ all night _____

Gtr. 1: w/ Rhy. Fig. 1
Gtr. 2 tacet   Gtr. 2: w/ Rhy. Fig. 1A, last 2 meas.   Gtrs. 1 & 2: w/ Rhy. Fig. 1A

E5

long, _____ ow! _____ All night long. _____

Verse

Gtrs. 1 & 2: w/ Rhy. Figs. 1 & 1A, 1st 3 meas.

E5   D5   A5   B5

2. Red light, green light, don't say no. _____ I real-ly want _____ her.

Gtrs. 1 & 2: w/ Rhy. Figs. 1 & 1A, 1st 3 meas.

E5   D5   A5   B5

She said, "Stop!" Ba-by, go, go, go! I real-ly want _____ her

Pre-Chorus

Gtrs. 1 & 2: w/ Rhy. Fig. 2
Gtr. 3: w/ Rhy. Fig. 2A

C#5   A5

by my side, the whole night through. _ We do all the things that we _____ wan-na do. _____ Well,

Gtr. 4 (elec.)

mf w/ dist.

full   full

6   7   7 5 4   6 4   6   4 6   5 6 4   5

C#5   A5   Gtr. 5 tacet   D5

come on, ba-by, don't leave me sad, _ 'cause you're good look-in', the best I've had. _ Mak-in' love, _

Gtr. 5 mf w/ dist. (elec.)   3   3

Gtr. 4
divisi   3   3

* full full

6   10/7 7 10/7 9/5 7/4   9/6 8/4   9/6   (6)   18 19 19 19 19

* Gtr. 4 to right of slashes in TAB.

81

Chorus
Gtrs. 1 & 2: w/ Rhy. Figs. 3 & 3A, 1 3/4 times
Gtrs. 3 & 4 tacet
E5
D5 A5 E5 D5
mak-in' love, mak-in' love all night long. Mak-in' love,
E5
D5 A5 open
Gtrs. 1 & 2
mak-in' love, mak-in' love all night.
Guitar Solo
Gtrs. 1 & 2: w/ Rhy. Figs. 1 & 1A, 3 3/4 times
E5
Gtr. 4
full
semi-Harm.
1 1/2
2

Whoa, ow!
8va
full
Chorus
Gtrs. 1 & 2: w/ Rhy. Figs. 3 & 3A
D5
E5
Gtrs. 1 & 2
Mak - in' love, mak - in' love, mak - in' love
play 1st time only
Gtr. 4 tacet
1., 2., 3.
4.
A5
all night long. Mak - in' love, night, ow!
Outro
Gtrs. 1 & 2: w/ Rhy. Figs. 3 & 3A, 1 3/4 times
Play 5 Times and Fade

from *Ace Frehley*

New York Groove

Words and Music by Russ Ballard

Verse

Gtr. 3 tacet
E

Gtr. 2

1. Man - y years since I was here. On the street, I was pass - in' my

Gtr. 1

B   A

time a - way. To the left and to the right, build-ings tow - er-ing to the sky. It's

E   B   **Pre-Chorus**
Gtrs. 1 & 2: w/ Rhy. Figs. 1 & 1A
E

out - ta sight in the dead of night.

Spoken: Here I am
(Oo.

Gtr. 3

and in this city, with a fist full of dollars, and baby, you better believe I'm

Oo. _____)

Chorus

Gtr. 3 tacet

Gtr. 2

| 1., 2. | 3. |

E   B   A   B   A   B

back, back in the New York groove. I'm groove.

Gtr. 1

wah-wah off

E

Gtr. 2

Back in the New York groove, in the New York groove.

Gtr. 3

Gtr. 1

w/ wah-wah

F

Rhy. Fig. 2A | End Rhy. Fig. 2A

Fill 1 | End Fill 1

Rhy. Fig. 2 | End Rhy. Fig. 2

Verse

Gtr. 3 tacet | Gtr. 3: w/ Fill 2

F

Gtr. 2

2. In the back _ of my Cad - il - lac,   wick-ed la - dy sit-tin' by   my   side, _ say-in',

Gtr. 1

Fill 2
Gtr. 3

"Where are we?" _ Stopped at Third __ and For - ty-three; ex - it to __ the right, it's gon-na be

ec - sta - sy. This place was meant for me. _

Pre-Chorus
Gtrs. 1 & 2: w/ Rhy. Fig. 2 & 2A, 2 times

Spoken: Feels so
(Oo. _____

good tonight. Who cares about tomorrow? So baby, you better believe I'm
_ Oo. _____)

Chorus
1., 2.
3.
Gtr. 3 tacet
Bkgd. Voc.: w/ Voc. Fig. 1
F C B♭ C B♭ C
Rhy. Fig. 3A
End Rhy. Fig. 3A
Gtr. 2
back, back in the New_York groove. I'm groove.
Gtr. 1
Rhy. Fig. 3
End Rhy. Fig. 3
wah-wah off
Outro-Chorus
Gtrs. 1 & 2: w/ Rhy. Figs. 3 & 3A
Bkgd. Voc.: w/ Voc. Fig. 1, 3rd time
Gtr. 3: w/ Fill 1
F C B♭ C
play 3 times
Back in the New York groove, in the New York groove. I'm back, back in the New_ York groove. I'm
Gtr. 3
w/ wah-wah
Play 4 Times and Fade
Gtrs. 1 & 2: w/ Rhy. Figs. 3 & 3A
Bkgd. Voc.: w/ Voc. Fig. 1
F C B♭ C
play 3 times
back, back in the New_ York groove. I'm back, back in the New_ York groove. I'm
Voc. Fig. 1
New York groove. New York groove.

from *Kiss*

Nothing to Lose

Words and Music by Gene Simmons

G   E5   F#   B   G^{III}

A5   A#5   B5   A5^{open}   E5^{open}

Tune Down 1/2 Step:
① = E♭ ④ = D♭
② = B♭ ⑤ = A♭
③ = G♭ ⑥ = E♭

Intro
Moderate Rock ♩ = 132

N.C.

play 4 times   Gtr. 2   G

1. Be -

Gtrs. 1 & 2
(dist.)

Riff A   **End Riff A**

(Gtr. 2 cont. in slash, 4th time)

mf

Verse   Gtr. 2 tacet   N.C.
E5

fore I had a ba - by, _____ I did-n't care an-y-way. _ I

Rhy. Fig. 1

E5   N.C.

thought a-bout the back   door, _____ I did-n't know what to say, _ yeah, _ yeah.   2. But

Gtr. 1   **End Rhy. Fig. 1**

Gtr. 2
divisi

Fill 1   **End Fill 1**

%§ **Verse**

Gtr. 1: w/ Rhy. Fig. 1
Gtr. 2 tacet, 1st time
Gtr. 2: w/ Rhy. Fill 1, 2nd time

E5   N.C.

once I got a ba - by,   I, I tried ev - 'ry way. _   She
now I've got a ba - by,   and we tried ev - 'ry way. _   Ya

E5   Gtr. 2: w/ Fill 1
                                            N.C.

did - n't wan - na do it,   ah, but she did an - y - way, ___ yeah, _ yeah.   But,
know, she wants to do it,   and she does an - y - way, ___ yeah, _ yeah.   Ya

Pre-Chorus

F#   B   F#   G^{III}

Gtr. 2

ba - by, please don't re - fuse, _   ya know you got noth-in' to lose. _____ You got noth-in' to lose. _

Gtr. 1

Chorus

A5   E5

Rhy. Fig. 2A   End Rhy. Fig. 2A

play 3 times

___ (You got,   got   noth-in' to lose. _   You got,   got   noth-in' to lose. _)

Rhy. Fig. 2   End Rhy. Fig. 2

* Lead voc. ad libs next 13 meas.

Rhy. Fill 1
Gtr. 2   play 5 times

91

To Coda
A5
A#5 B5
N.C.
(Cont. in notation)
You got, got, you got, you got, you got noth-in' to lose.
Gtrs. 1 & 2
D.S. al Coda
3. So
Coda
Guitar Solo
Gtr. 1: w/ Rhy. Fig. 3, 2 times
E5
A5 open
you got noth - in' to lose.
Gtr. 3 (dist.)
f
full
Rhy. Fig. 3
Gtr. 1
T
A
B

Outro-Chorus

Gtr. 3 tacet
w/ Lead Voc. ad Libs, till fade

Gtrs. 1 & 2 tacet

(You got, got noth-in' to lose. _ You got, got noth-in' to lose. _

piano enters

You got, got noth-in' to lose. _ You got, got noth-in' to lose. _

Gtrs. 1 & 2: w/ Rhy. Figs. 2 & 2A, simile

Play 4 Times and Fade

You got, got noth-in' to lose. _ You got, got noth-in' to lose. _)

from *Dressed to Kill*

Rock Bottom

Words and Music by Paul Stanley and Ace Frehley

Tune Down 1/2 Step:

① = E♭ ④ = D♭
② = B♭ ⑤ = A♭
③ = G♭ ⑥ = E♭

Prelude

Moderately ♩. = 90

* Chord symbols reflect implied tonality.

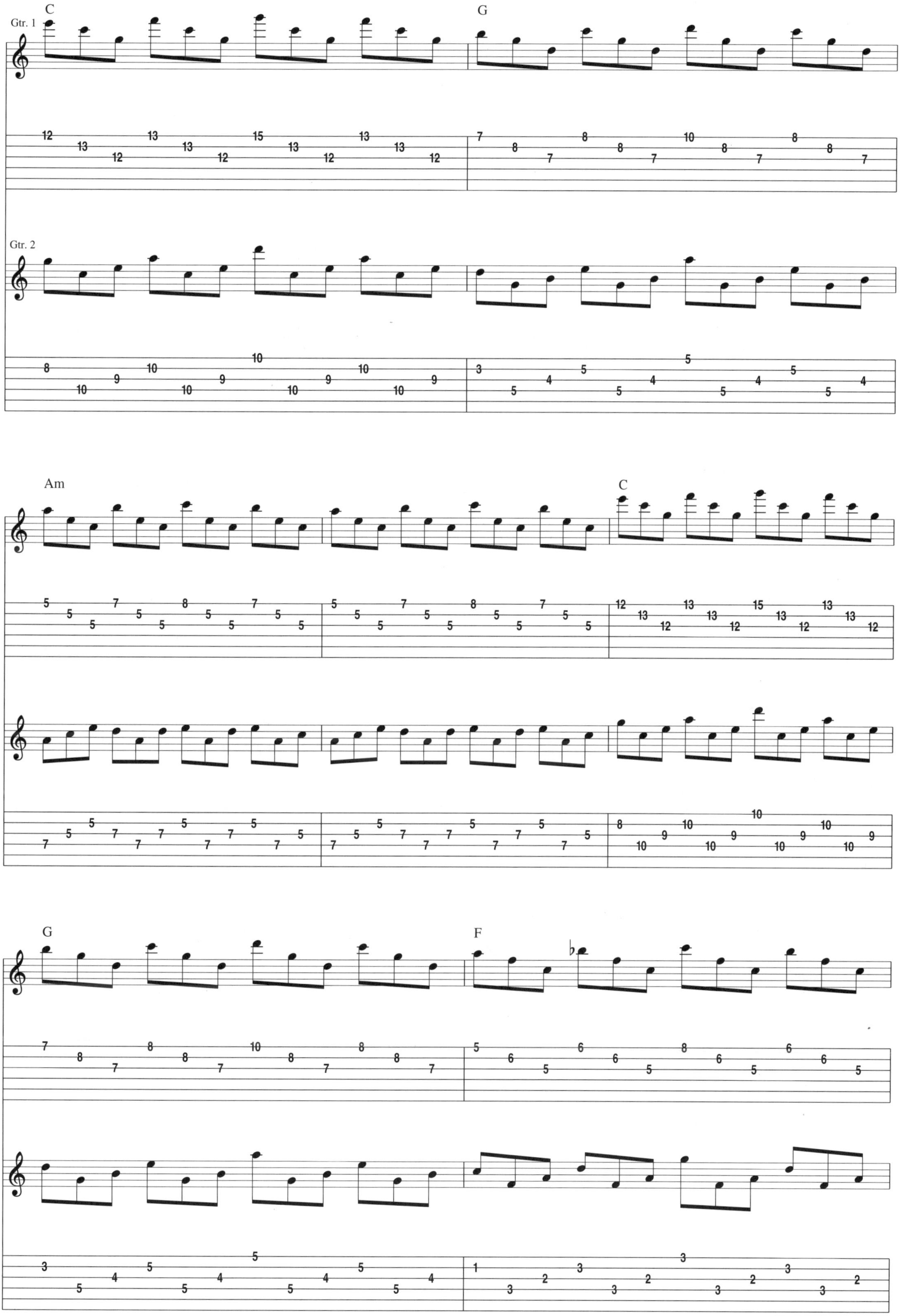
Gtr. 1
Gtr. 2
C
G
Am
C
G
F

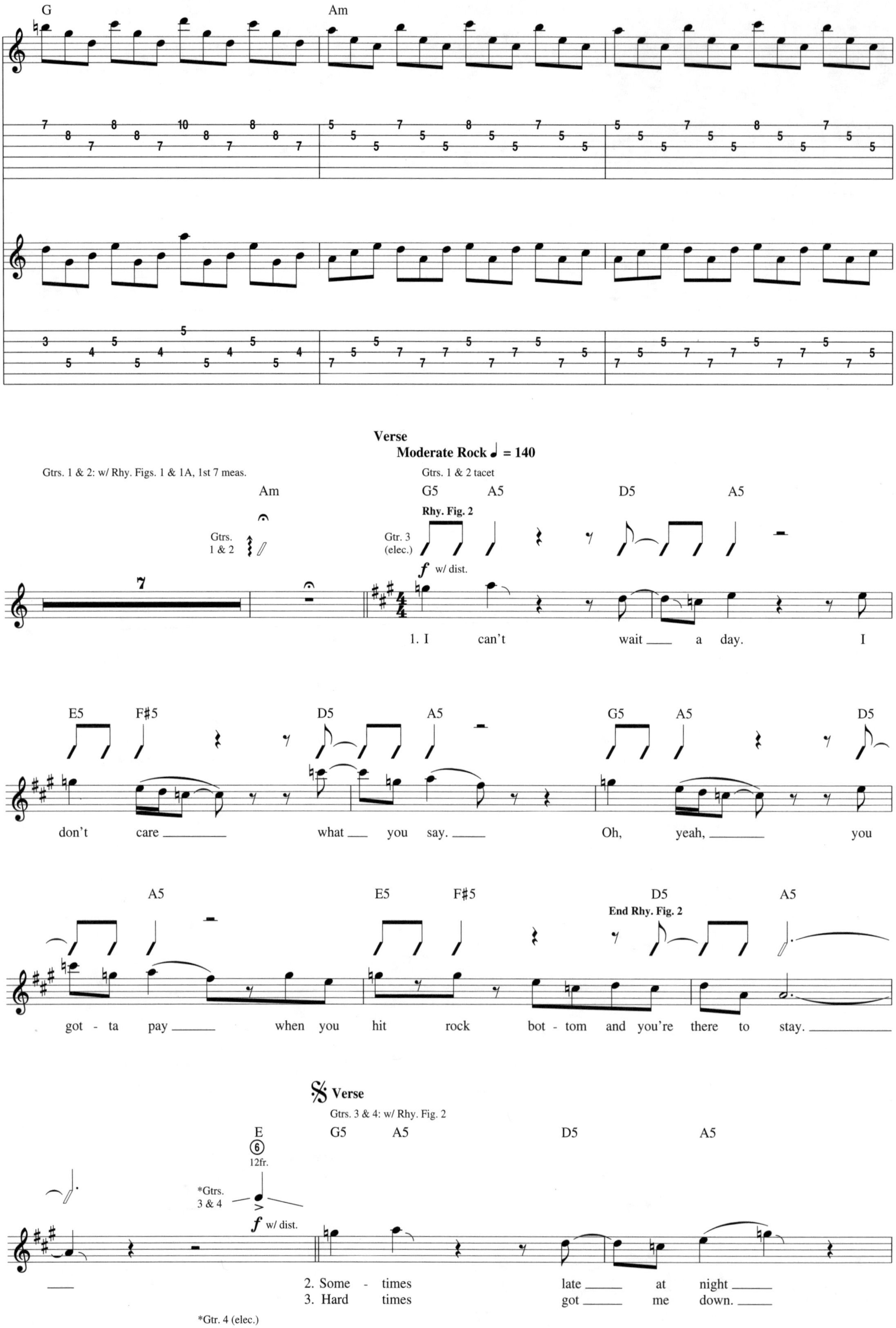
G
Am
Verse
Moderate Rock ♩ = 140
Gtrs. 1 & 2: w/ Rhy. Figs. 1 & 1A, 1st 7 meas.
Gtrs. 1 & 2 tacet
Am
G5 A5 D5 A5
Rhy. Fig. 2
Gtrs. 1 & 2
Gtr. 3 (elec.)
w/ dist.
1. I can't wait a day. I
E5 F#5 D5 A5 G5 A5 D5
don't care what you say. Oh, yeah, you
A5 E5 F#5 D5 A5
End Rhy. Fig. 2
got - ta pay when you hit rock bot - tom and you're there to stay.
Verse
Gtrs. 3 & 4: w/ Rhy. Fig. 2
E G5 A5 D5 A5
12fr.
*Gtrs. 3 & 4
w/ dist.
2. Some - times late at night
3. Hard times got me down.
*Gtr. 4 (elec.)

E5 F#5 D5 A5 G5 A5 D5
I want to hold you tight. Oh, no, you
Good times ain't a - round. Now I got a
A5 E5 F#5 D5 A5 D5 A5
Gtrs. 3 & 4
(Gtr. 4 cont. in notation)
got - ta pay. lot to say. Girl, you hit rock bot - tom and you're there to stay.
Chorus
B5 B7/A B5 B7/A B5 D5V E5VII B7/A B5 B7/A B5 D5V
Rhy. Fig. 3
Gtr. 3
Rock bot - tom. Girl, you know you ought to treat me good.
Rhy. Fig. 3A
Gtr. 4
B5 B7/A B5 B7/A B5 D5V A5
To Coda E5VII
End Rhy. Fig. 3
Rock bot - tom. Oh, you nev - er treat me like you should.
End Rhy. Fig. 3A
Guitar Solo
Gtrs. 3 & 4: w/ Rhy. Fig. 2
G5 A5 D5 A5 E5 F#5 D5
Gtr. 5 (elec.)
f w/ dist.
full
full
full

A5
G5 A5
D5
A5
full
1/4
1 1/2
E5
F♯5
D5
A5
D.S. al Coda
Gtrs. 3 & 4
full
Coda
Gtrs. 3 & 4: w/ Rhy. Figs. 3 & 3A
B5
B7/A B5 B7/A B5
E5
B7/A
(Rock bot - tom.)
Girl, you know you ought to treat me good.
B5 B7/A B5
Rock bot - tom.
Yeah, you nev - er treat me like you should.
Gtrs. 3 & 4: w/ Rhy. Figs. 3 & 3A, 1st 5 meas.
(Rock bot - tom.)
Gtr. 3
Ow!
Gtr. 4

Rocket Ride

Words and Music by Ace Frehley and S. Delaney

F#5 G5 G#5 A5 A#5 B5

C5 C#5 B5 II E5 C5 III D5

E5 VII F#5 IX B5 IX D5 X D#5 E5 XII A5 XII

Tune Down 1/2 Step:

① = Eb   ④ = Db
② = Bb   ⑤ = Ab
③ = Gb   ⑥ = Eb

Intro
Moderate Rock ♩ = 146

Gtrs. 1 & 2 (dist.)   F#5   G5   G#5   A5   A#5   B5   C5   C#5

mf w/ flanger

(cont. in notation)

Gtrs. 1 & 2   **Riff A**   N.C.   **End Riff A**

Gtr. 2   **Riff B**   **End Riff B**

(cont. in slash)

Gtr. 1   **Riff B1**   **End Riff B1**

(cont. in slash)

Verse

1. La - dy space, you like the way ___ I make you feel in - side. ___
2. La - dy space, you bet - ter wake up fast. Count-down is com - in' on.

Take a rock - et ride.
Take a rock - et ride.

From the start you want - ed to fly. ___ I got the rock - et, and
The grav - i - ty that used to hold you down just don't ex - ist no more.

you want the ride. ___ Take a rock - et ride.
Take a rock - et ride.

Ba -

Chorus

- by wants it fast, ba - by wants a blast. She wants a rock - et ride, she wants a rock - et ride. Ba -

Fill 1
Gtr. 2

100

- by wants it fast, ba - by wants a blast. She wants a rock-et ride, she wants a rock-et ride.

Interlude

Come on, grab a hold of my rocket!

* Microphonic fdbk., not caused by str. vibration.

** Gtr. 2 turns flanger off.

* Played slightly ahead of the beat

Chorus

Gtrs. 1 & 2: w/ Rhy. Fig. 2, 1st 4 meas.
Gtr. 3 tacet

- by wants it fast, ba - by wants a blast. She wants a rock-et ride, she wants a rock-et ride. Ba -

Gtrs. 1 & 2: w/ Rhy. Fig. 2

- by's on her knees, ba - by wants to please. She wants a rock-et ride, she wants a rock-et ride. Ba -

- by's on her knees, ba - by wants to please. She wants a rock-et ride, she wants a rock-et ride.

Outro

Gtrs. 1 & 2: w/ Riff A   Gtrs. 1 & 2: w/ Riffs B & B1, 1st 3 meas.

N.C.
Gtr. 2

Gtr. 1
* *divisi*

(cont. in slash)

14/7 12/5
14/7 13/6 12/5
14/7 13/6 12/5

* Gtr. 1 to right of slash in TAB.

Free Time

Gtrs.
1 & 2

Gtr. 3

wah-wah off

full   full   1/2

Gtrs. 1 & 2 tacet

1/2

Gtr. 3 tacet

(drums)

full   full

Gtrs.   A5/E
1 & 2

8va

loco

fdbk.

pitch: G

from *Alive II*

Rockin' in the U.S.A.

Words and Music by Gene Simmons

Tune Down 1/2 Step:
① = Eb ④ = Db
② = Bb ⑤ = Ab
③ = Gb ⑥ = Eb

Intro
Moderate Rock ♩ = 150

*E

Gtr. 2 (dist.)   Riff A

Gtr. 1 (dist.)   Riff A1

P.M. P.M. P.M.   P.M. P.M.   P.M. P.M. P.M.   P.M. P.M.

* Chord symbols reflect implied tonality.

1. I'm

End Riff A1

(cont. in slash)

End Riff A

P.M. P.M. P.M.   P.M. P.M.   P.M. P.M. P.M.   P.M. P.M.

Verse

Gtr. 1: w/ Riff A

Gtr. 2

fly - in' in a Sev - en For - ty - Sev - en. I'm pass - in' by the pearl - y gates.

(cont. in notation)

And I'm com - in' real close to Heav - en, and my gui - tar just can't wait,

Chorus
Gtr. 3: w/ Fill 1
B E E6 E5 E6 E5 C5 D5 E
is rock - in' in the U. S. A. No -
End Rhy. Fill 2
Rhy. Fig. 1
Gtr. 1
Rhy. Fig. 1A
Gtr. 2
E6 E5 E6 E5 C5 D5 E N.C. E5
- where else I'd rath - er stay. Rock - in' and a - roll - in', rock -

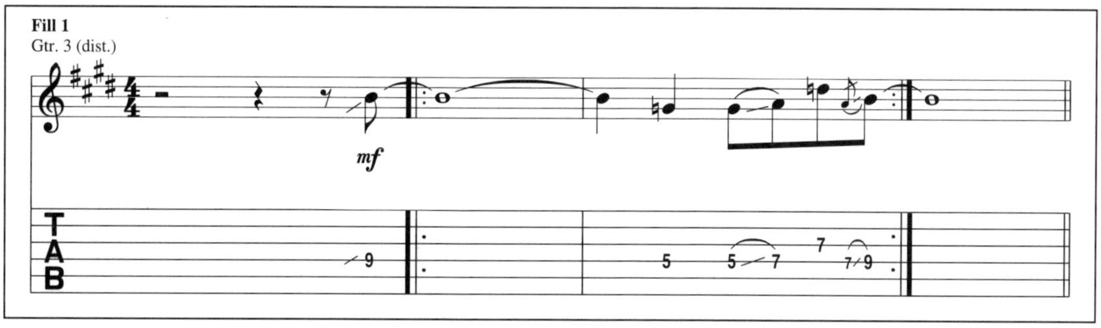
Fill 1
Gtr. 3 (dist.)
mf
T
A
B

N.C. E5 N.C. D E
- in' and a - roll - in', rock - in' in the U. S. A.
End Rhy. Fig. 1
Gtr. 3
Gtr. 1
divisi
End Rhy. Fig. 1A
Guitar Solo
Gtrs. 1 & 2: w/ Riffs A & A1
Gtr. 3
E
1/2
full
Gtrs. 1 & 2: w/ Rhy. Fills 1 & 1A
A D/F♯ A E
3. Ger -
Verse
Gtrs. 1 & 2: w/ Riffs A & A1
E
- man - y was real - ly neat.
Ja - pan had much to eat.

And Den-mark was great, ___ but I just can't wait, ___ rock-in' the U. S. A. ___

Gtrs. 1 & 2: w/ Rhy. Fills 1 & 1A, 1st meas.

Gtrs. 1 & 2: w/ Rhy. Fill 2

A   D/F#   A   B

Outro-Chorus

Gtr. 3 tacet

* Gtrs. 1 & 2: w/ Rhy. Figs. 1 & 1A

E/G#   B   E   C5   D5   E

Rock - in' in the U. S.   A. ___   No -
(Rock - in' in the U. S.   A. ___

* Play 1st 6 meas., 4th time

C5   D5   E   N.C.

- where else I'd ___ rath - er stay. ___   Rock - in' and a - roll - in',   rock-
Rock - in' in the U. S.   A. ___   Rock - in' and roll -

1., 2., 3.

D

- in' and a - roll - in',   rock - in' in the U. S.   A. ___
- in',   rock - in' and roll - in'.)

E ‖4.   C   D   E

Rock - in', in the U. S.   U. ___   S. ___   A. ___
- in'.)

Gtrs. 1 & 2   Gtr. 2   Gtrs. 1 & 2

Gtr. 1
* divisi

* Gtr. 1 to right of slash in TAB.

109

from *Alive II*

Shock Me

Words and Music by Ace Frehley

Tune Down 1/2 Step:
① = Eb ④ = Db
② = Bb ⑤ = Ab
③ = Gb ⑥ = Eb

Intro
Moderate Rock ♩ = 132

1. Your light-ning's all I need. My sat-is-fac-tion grows. _____
2. And ba-by, if you do _ what you've been told. _____

You _____ make me feel at ease, _ you e-ven make me glow. _____
My in-su-la-tion's gone, girl, _ you make me o-ver-load.

Pre-Chorus
A5 A5 B5 A5 B5 A5 B5 E5 F#5 E5 F#5 E5 F#5 D
Don't cut the pow-er on me. I'm feel-ing low, so get me
Don't pull the plug on me, no, no. Keep it in, and keep me
1/2
* Played by Gtr. 2 only.
Chorus
C B A5 *G5/A D C
high. Shock me.
high.
(Make me feel bet-ter.)
Rhy. Fig. 2
End Rhy. Fig. 2
* bass plays A
Gtrs. 1 & 2: w/ Rhy. Fig. 2, 1 1/2 times
A5 *G5/A D C A5 *G5/A
Shock me. Shock me.
(Put on your black leath-er.) (We
* bass plays A
*bass plays A
1.
D E
Gtrs. 1 & 2
(cont. in notation)
can come to-geth-er.)
Interlude
Gtrs. 1 & 2
D/A A D/A A D/A A G5 D/A G/A D/A N.C. A5
1/2
1/2
1/2
1/2

2.
D
E
Gtr. 1
Come on.
Gtr. 2
Guitar Solo
Gtr. 1: w/ Rhy. Fig. 1, 4 times
D/A A
D/A A
D/A A
G5
D/A
G/A D/A
N.C.
8va
loco
full
A5
D/A A
D/A A
D/A
A
G5
D/A
G/A
D/A
N.C.
A5

D/A A D/A A D/A A G5
8va
1 1/2
D/A G/A D/A N.C. A5 D/A A D/A A
full
D/A A G5 D/A G/A D/A N.C.
A5 A5 B5 A5 B5 A5 B5 A5 B5 A5
Rhy. Fig. 3
End Rhy. Fig. 3
Gtr. 1
loco
steady gliss.
semi-harm.
Gtr. 1: w/ Rhy. Fig. 3, 3 times
B5 A5 B5 A5 B5 A5 B5 A5 B5 A5 B5 A5
full 1/2

Chorus

Gtr. 1: w/ Rhy. Fig. 2, 1st 2 meas., 3 times

Shock me. __
(Ba - by. __)

Shock me. __
(Whoa, yeah. __)

Shock me. __
(Ba - by. __)

fdbk.

pitch: E
* bass plays A

Gtrs. 1 & 2: w/ Rhy. Fig. 2

Chorus

Gtrs. 1 & 2: w/ Rhy. Fig. 2, 4 times

Shock me. ____
(Whoa, yeah. ____)

* bass plays A

Shock me. ____
(Make __

__ me feel bet-ter.

Whoa, yeah. __

I'm down to the bare wire. __ Shock me. __

Put on __ your black leath- er.

* bass plays A

Lyrics (below staves):

I wan-na feel your pow-er. Shock me.___
We ___ can come to-geth-er. Whoa, yeah.___

Ba - by.___

* bass plays A

Come on, come on and shock me.___
We ___ can come to-geth-er. Whoa, yeah._____)

___

* bass plays A

Interlude

A5 open   C5/G

Gtr. 1

Gtr. 2 **Riff A**   **End Riff A**

Outro Guitar Solo
Gtr. 1: w/ Riff A, 4 times

G
④
5 fr

N.C.(A5)   C5/G   N.C.(A5)   D5/A

Gtr. 2

N.C.(A5)   C5/G N.C.(A5)   D5/A   N.C.(A5)   C5/G N.C.(A5)   D5/A

full   full   full   full   full   full

N.C.(A5)
C5/G
N.C.(A5)
D5/A
Free Time
A
open
Gtr. 1
full
Gtr. 1 tacet
N.C.
w/ echo repeats
8va
loco
P.H.
grad. bend
1/2
fdbk.
pitch: B♭

* Tap w/ edge of pick.

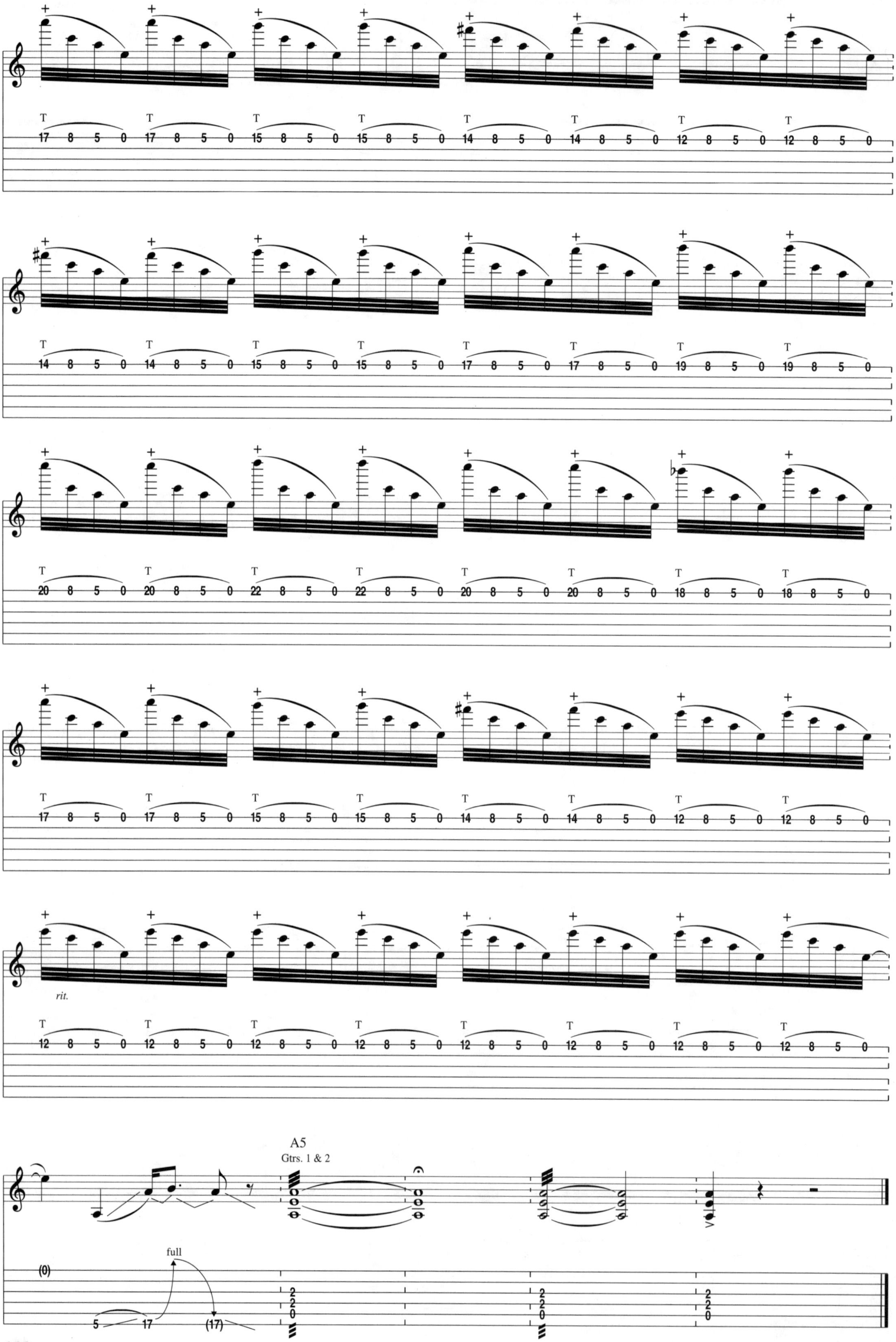
rit.
A5
Gtrs. 1 & 2
full

from *Revenge*

Unholy

Words and Music by Gene Simmons and Vinnie Vincent

Tune Down 1/2 Step:
① = Eb ④ = Db
② = Bb ⑤ = Ab
③ = Gb ⑥ = Eb

Intro

Moderate Rock ♩ = 120

N.C.

(misc. gtr. sounds)

(approx. 18 sec.)

1. I was

(misc. gtr. sounds) Gtrs. 1 & 2 (dist.)

(approx. 18 sec.)

mf

P.H.   P.H.

Verse

N.C.

there through the ag - es, chained slaves to their ca - ges. I have seen you eat your own._

P.H.

A5   D5/A C5/G G5/D N.C.(F5) (Bb5) (A5)   (Ab5)

I'm the cy - cle of pain _ of a thou - sand year old reign._ I'm su - i -

P.H.

N.C.
cide and sal - va - tion, the o - men to na - tions that you wor - ship on all fours.
Riff A
P.H.
C5 B5 N.C. Eb5 D5
I'm the in - fec - tion and fam - ine that's knock - ing at your door.
End Riff A
P.H.
P.M.
Chorus
D5/A C5/G D5/A C5/G N.C. C5 B5
That's why you're feel - ing so un - ho - ly.
Riff B
N.C. C5 B5
Oh, I was cre - at - ed by man. You know I'm un - ho - ly.
End Riff B

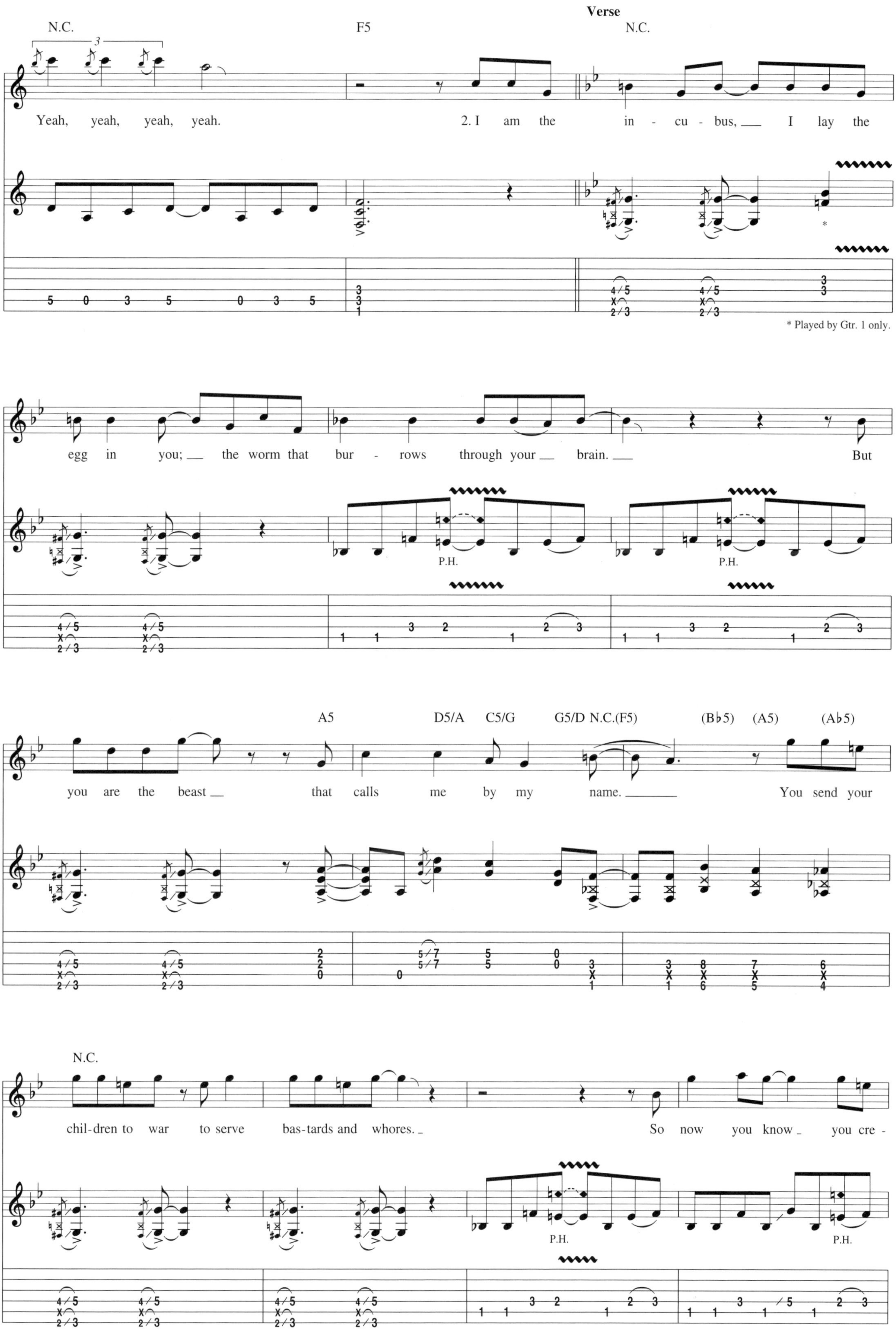

* Played by Gtr. 1 only.

C5 B5 N.C. E♭5 D5 D5/A C5/G
at - ed me on the day that you were born.
P.M.
P.M.
Chorus
Gtrs. 1 & 2: w/ Riff B, 2 3/4 times
N.C. C5 B5 N.C.
Un - ho - ly. I was cre - at - ed by man, yeah, I'm the
C5 B5 N.C.
lord of the flies. You know I'm un - ho - ly. From the left hand of pow - er comes the
C5 B5 N.C.
fa - ther of lies, yeah. Un - ho - ly. Un - ho - ly.
Interlude
N.C. G5/D F♯5/C♯ N.C.
Gtr. 3 (dist.)
mf
string noise
Gtrs. 1 & 2
Gtr. 1
Gtr. 2
divisi
Riff C
Gtrs. 1 & 2
Gtr. 1
End Riff C
Gtr. 2
divisi
Guitar Solo
Gtrs. 1 & 2: w/ Riff C, 3 times
N.C. G5/D F♯5/C♯
Gtr. 3
f
w/ bar
-1

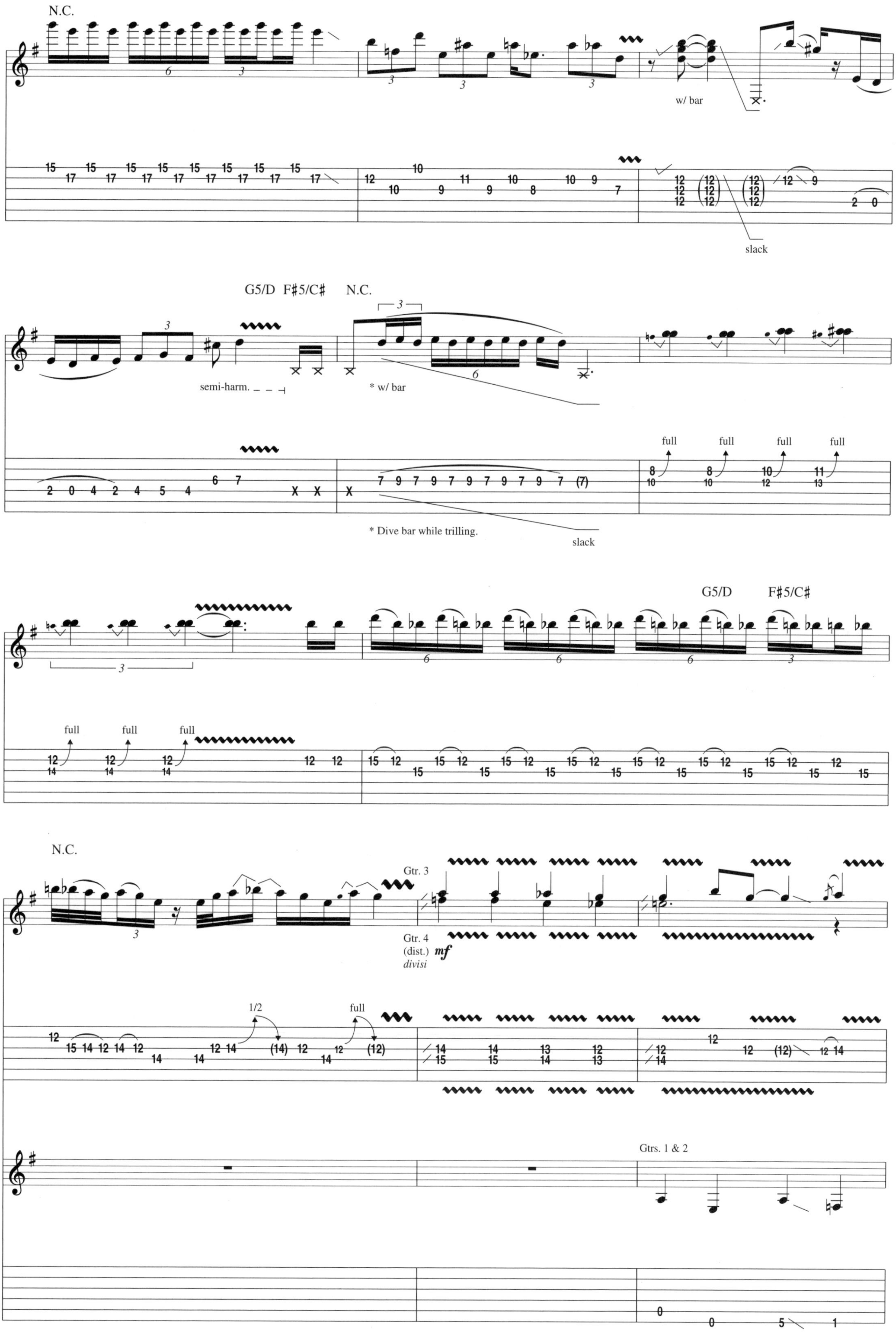
N.C.
w/ bar
slack
G5/D F♯5/C♯ N.C.
semi-harm.
* w/ bar
full
* Dive bar while trilling.
slack
G5/D F♯5/C♯
N.C.
Gtr. 3
Gtr. 4
(dist.) mf
divisi
1/2
full
Gtrs. 1 & 2

Gtr. 4 tacet
3. I lay you
Gtr. 3
8va
full
Gtrs. 1 & 2
Verse
Gtrs. 1 & 2: w/ Riff A
N.C.
down to sleep, your soul to keep. Bet - ter cross your heart be - fore you die. And
w/ bar
steady gliss.
loco
Gtrs. 1 & 2: w/ Fill 1
C5 B5 N.C. E♭5 D5 N.C. D5/A C5/G D5/A C5/G
now you know, know that you are mine. That's why you're feel - ing so
P.H.
Harm. w/ bar
1/2
pitch: C♯ C♯ F F♯
A, D
slack
Fill 1
Gtrs. 1 & 2
P.M.
T
A
B

Outro-Chorus

Gtrs. 1 & 2: w/ Riff B, 3 times
Gtr. 3 tacet

125

Guitar Notation Legend

Guitar Music can be notated three different ways: on a *musical staff*, in *tablature*, and in *rhythm slashes*.

RHYTHM SLASHES are written above the staff. Strum chords in the rhythm indicated. Use the chord diagrams found at the top of the first page of the transcription for the appropriate chord voicings. Round noteheads indicate single notes.

THE MUSICAL STAFF shows pitches and rhythms and is divided by bar lines into measures. Pitches are named after the first seven letters of the alphabet.

TABLATURE graphically represents the guitar fingerboard. Each horizontal line represents a a string, and each number represents a fret.

4th string, 2nd fret

1st & 2nd strings open, played together

open D chord

Definitions for Special Guitar Notation

HALF-STEP BEND: Strike the note and bend up 1/2 step.

WHOLE-STEP BEND: Strike the note and bend up one step.

GRACE NOTE BEND: Strike the note and bend up as indicated. The first note does not take up any time.

SLIGHT (MICROTONE) BEND: Strike the note and bend up 1/4 step.

BEND AND RELEASE: Strike the note and bend up as indicated, then release back to the original note. Only the first note is struck.

PRE-BEND: Bend the note as indicated, then strike it.

PRE-BEND AND RELEASE: Bend the note as indicated. Strike it and release the bend back to the original note.

UNISON BEND: Strike the two notes simultaneously and bend the lower note up to the pitch of the higher.

VIBRATO: The string is vibrated by rapidly bending and releasing the note with the fretting hand.

WIDE VIBRATO: The pitch is varied to a greater degree by vibrating with the fretting hand.

HAMMER-ON: Strike the first (lower) note with one finger, then sound the higher note (on the same string) with another finger by fretting it without picking.

PULL-OFF: Place both fingers on the notes to be sounded. Strike the first note and without picking, pull the finger off to sound the second (lower) note.

LEGATO SLIDE: Strike the first note and then slide the same fret-hand finger up or down to the second note. The second note is not struck.

SHIFT SLIDE: Same as legato slide, except the second note is struck.

TRILL: Very rapidly alternate between the notes indicated by continuously hammering on and pulling off.

TAPPING: Hammer ("tap") the fret indicated with the pick-hand index or middle finger and pull off to the note fretted by the fret hand.

NATURAL HARMONIC: Strike the note while the fret-hand lightly touches the string directly over the fret indicated.

Harm.

TAB 12

PINCH HARMONIC: The note is fretted normally and a harmonic is produced by adding the edge of the thumb or the tip of the index finger of the pick hand to the normal pick attack.

P.H.

TAB 5

HARP HARMONIC: The note is fretted normally and a harmonic is produced by gently resting the pick hand's index finger directly above the indicated fret (in parentheses) while the pick hand's thumb or pick assists by plucking the appropriate string.

8va

H.H.

TAB 7(19)

PICK SCRAPE: The edge of the pick is rubbed down (or up) the string, producing a scratchy sound.

P.S.

TAB

MUFFLED STRINGS: A percussive sound is produced by laying the fret hand across the string(s) without depressing, and striking them with the pick hand.

TAB X X

PALM MUTING: The note is partially muted by the pick hand lightly touching the string(s) just before the bridge.

P.M.

TAB 0 0 0 0

RAKE: Drag the pick across the strings indicated with a single motion.

rake

TAB 5 X X

TREMOLO PICKING: The note is picked as rapidly and continuously as possible.

TAB 5 7

ARPEGGIATE: Play the notes of the chord indicated by quickly rolling them from bottom to top.

TAB 5 5 5

VIBRATO BAR DIVE AND RETURN: The pitch of the note or chord is dropped a specified number of steps (in rhythm) then returned to the original pitch.

w/ bar

TAB 0 (0)

-1

VIBRATO BAR SCOOP: Depress the bar just before striking the note, then quickly release the bar.

w/ bar

TAB 4 5 7

VIBRATO BAR DIP: Strike the note and then immediately drop a specified number of steps, then release back to the original pitch.

-1/2 -1/2 -1/2

w/ bar
-1/2 -1/2 -1/2

TAB 7 7 7

Additional Musical Definitions

>	(accent)	• Accentuate note (play it louder)
∧	(accent)	• Accentuate note with great intensity
.	(staccato)	• Play the note short
⊓		• Downstroke
∨		• Upstroke
D.S. al Coda		• Go back to the sign (𝄉), then play until the measure marked "**To Coda**," then skip to the section labelled "**Coda**."
D.S. al Fine		• Go back to the beginning of the song and play until the measure marked "**Fine**" (end).

Rhy. Fig.	• Label used to recall a recurring accompaniment pattern (usually chordal).
Riff	• Label used to recall composed, melodic lines (usually single notes) which recur.
Fill	• Label used to identify a brief melodic figure which is to be inserted into the arrangement.
Rhy. Fill	• A chordal version of a Fill.
tacet	• Instrument is silent (drops out).
	• Repeat measures between signs.
1. 2.	• When a repeated section has different endings, play the first ending only the first time and the second ending only the second time.

NOTE: Tablature numbers in parentheses mean:
1. The note is being sustained over a system (note in standard notation is tied), or
2. The note is sustained, but a new articulation (such as a hammer-on, pull-off, slide or vibrato begins, or
3. The note is a barely audible "ghost" note (note in standard notation is also in parentheses).

RECORDED VERSIONS
The Best Note-For-Note Transcriptions Available

GUITAR

ALL BOOKS INCLUDE TABLATURE

00690002 Aerosmith – Big Ones	$24.95
00694909 Aerosmith – Get A Grip	$19.95
00660133 Aerosmith – Pump	$19.95
00690139 Alice In Chains	$19.95
00694865 Alice In Chains – Dirt	$19.95
00660225 Alice In Chains – Facelift	$19.95
00694925 Alice In Chains – Jar Of Flies/Sap	$19.95
00694932 Allman Brothers Band – Volume 1	$24.95
00694933 Allman Brothers Band – Volume 2	$24.95
00694934 Allman Brothers Band – Volume 3	$24.95
00690158 Chet Atkins – Almost Alone	$19.95
00694877 Chet Atkins – Guitars For All Seasons	$19.95
00694918 Randy Bachman Collection	$22.95
00694929 Beatles: 1962-1966	$24.95
00694930 Beatles: 1967-1970	$24.95
00694880 Beatles – Abbey Road	$19.95
00690044 Beatles – Live At The BBC	$22.95
00694891 Beatles – Revolver	$19.95
00694914 Beatles – Rubber Soul	$19.95
00694863 Beatles – Sgt. Pepper's Lonely Hearts Club Band	$19.95
00690174 Beck – Mellow Gold	$17.95
00690175 Beck – Odelay	$17.95
00694931 Belly – Star	$19.95
00694884 The Best of George Benson	$19.95
00692385 Chuck Berry	$19.95
00692200 Black Sabbath – We Sold Our Soul For Rock 'N' Roll	$19.95
00690115 Blind Melon – Soup	$19.95
00690028 Blue Oyster Cult – Cult Classics	$19.95
00690102 Bon Jovi – These Days	$24.95
00690173 Tracy Bonham – The Burdens Of Being Upright	$19.95
00694935 Boston: Double Shot Of	$22.95
00690043 Cheap Trick – Best Of	$19.95
00306124 Chicago – The Retrospective Collection	$22.95
00694875 Eric Clapton – Boxed Set	$75.00
00692392 Eric Clapton – Crossroads Vol. 1	$22.95
00692393 Eric Clapton – Crossroads Vol. 2	$22.95
00692394 Eric Clapton – Crossroads Vol. 3	$22.95
00690010 Eric Clapton – From The Cradle	$19.95
00660139 Eric Clapton – Journeyman	$19.95
00694869 Eric Clapton – Live Acoustic	$19.95
00694873 Eric Clapton – Timepieces	$19.95
00694896 John Mayall/Eric Clapton – Bluesbreakers	$19.95
00694837 Albert Collins – The Complete Imperial Records	$19.95
00694941 Crash Test Dummies – God Shuffled His Feet	$19.95
00694840 Cream – Disraeli Gears	$19.95
00690007 Danzig 4	$19.95
00690184 DC Talk – Jesus Freak	$19.95
00660186 Alex De Grassi Guitar Collection	$19.95
00694831 Derek And The Dominos – Layla & Other Assorted Love Songs	$19.95
00690187 Dire Straits – Brothers In Arms	$19.95
00690191 Dire Straits – Money For Nothing	$24.95
00690182 Dishwalla – Pet Your Friends	$19.95
00660178 Willie Dixon – Master Blues Composer	$24.95
00690089 Foo Fighters	$19.95
00690042 Robben Ford Blues Collection	$19.95
00694920 Free – Best Of	$18.95
00694894 Frank Gambale – The Great Explorers	$19.95
00694807 Danny Gatton – 88 Elmira St	$19.95
00690127 Goo Goo Dolls – A Boy Named Goo	$19.95
00690117 John Gorka Collection	$19.95
00690114 Buddy Guy Collection Vol. A-J	$19.95

00690193 Buddy Guy Collection Vol. L-Y	$19.95
00694798 George Harrison Anthology	$19.95
00690068 Return Of The Hellecasters	$19.95
00692930 Jimi Hendrix – Are You Experienced?	$19.95
00692931 Jimi Hendrix – Axis: Bold As Love	$19.95
00694944 Jimi Hendrix – Blues	$24.95
00660192 The Jimi Hendrix – Concerts	$24.95
00692932 Jimi Hendrix – Electric Ladyland	$24.95
00660099 Jimi Hendrix – Radio One	$24.95
00694919 Jimi Hendrix – Stone Free	$19.95
00690017 Jimi Hendrix – Woodstock	$24.95
00690038 Gary Hoey – Best Of	$19.95
00660029 Buddy Holly	$19.95
00660200 John Lee Hooker – The Healer	$19.95
00660169 John Lee Hooker – A Blues Legend	$19.95
00690054 Hootie & The Blowfish – Cracked Rear View	$19.95
00690143 Hootie & The Blowfish – Fairweather Johnson	$19.95
00694905 Howlin' Wolf	$19.95
00690136 Indigo Girls – 1200 Curfews	$19.95
00694938 Elmore James – Master Electric Slide Guitar	$19.95
00694833 Billy Joel For Guitar	$19.95
00694912 Eric Johnson – Ah Via Musicom	$19.95
00694911 Eric Johnson – Tones	$19.95
00690169 Eric Johnson – Venus Isle	$19.95
00694799 Robert Johnson – At The Crossroads	$19.95
00693185 Judas Priest – Vintage Hits	$19.95
00690073 B. B. King – 1950-1957	$24.95
00690098 B. B. King – 1958-1967	$24.95
00690099 B. B. King – 1962-1971	$24.95
00690019 King's X – Best Of	$19.95
00694903 The Best Of Kiss	$24.95
00690163 Mark Knopfler/Chet Atkins – Neck and Neck	$19.95
00690070 Live – Throwing Copper	$19.95
00690018 Living Colour – Best Of	$19.95
00694954 Lynyrd Skynyrd, New Best Of	$19.95
00694845 Yngwie Malmsteen – Fire And Ice	$19.95
00690190 Marilyn Manson – Antichrist Superstar	$19.95
00694956 Bob Marley – Legend	$19.95
00690075 Bob Marley – Natural Mystic	$19.95
00690020 Meat Loaf – Bat Out Of Hell I & II	$22.95
00694951 Megadeth – Rust In Peace	$22.95
00690011 Megadeth – Youthanasia	$19.95
00690040 Steve Miller Band Greatest Hits	$19.95
00694868 Gary Moore – After Hours	$19.95
00694802 Gary Moore – Still Got The Blues	$19.95
00690103 Alanis Morissette – Jagged Little Pill	$19.95
00694958 Mountain, Best Of	$19.95
00694895 Nirvana – Bleach	$19.95
00690189 Nirvana – From The Muddy Banks of the Wishkah	$19.95
00694913 Nirvana – In Utero	$19.95
00694901 Nirvana – Incesticide	$19.95
00694883 Nirvana – Nevermind	$19.95
00690026 Nirvana – Unplugged In New York	$19.95
00690159 Oasis – Definitely Maybe	$19.95
00690121 Oasis – (What's The Story) Morning Glory	$19.95
00694830 Ozzy Osbourne – No More Tears	$19.95
00690129 Ozzy Osbourne – Ozzmosis	$22.95
00694855 Pearl Jam – Ten	$19.95
00690053 Liz Phair – Whip Smart	$19.95
00690176 Phish – Billy Breathes	$22.95
00693800 Pink Floyd – Early Classics	$19.95
00694967 Police – Message In A Box Boxed Set	$70.00

00690032 Elvis Presley – The Sun Sessions	$22.95
00694974 Queen – A Night At The Opera	$19.95
00694969 Queensryche – Selections from "Operation: Mindcrime"	$19.95
00694910 Rage Against The Machine	$19.95
00690145 Rage Against The Machine – Evil Empire	$19.95
00690055 Red Hot Chili Peppers – Bloodsugarsexmagik	$19.95
00690090 Red Hot Chili Peppers – One Hot Minute	$22.95
00690027 Red Hot Chili Peppers – Out In L.A.	$19.95
00694968 Red Hot Chili Peppers – Selections from "What Hits!?"	$22.95
00694892 Guitar Style Of Jerry Reed	$19.95
00694937 Jimmy Reed – Master Bluesman	$19.95
00694899 R.E.M. – Automatic For The People	$19.95
00694898 R.E.M. – Out Of Time	$19.95
00690014 Rolling Stones – Exile On Main Street	$24.95
00690186 Rolling Stones – Rock & Roll Circus	$19.95
00694976 Rolling Stones – Some Girls	$24.95
00690133 Rusted Root – When I Woke	$19.95
00694836 Richie Sambora – Stranger In This Town	$19.95
00690031 Santana's Greatest Hits	$19.95
00694805 Scorpions – Crazy World	$19.95
00694916 Scorpions – Face The Heat	$19.95
00690128 Seven Mary Three – American Standards	$19.95
00690076 Sex Pistols – Never Mind The Bollocks	$19.95
00690130 Silverchair – Frogstomp	$19.95
00690041 Smithereens – Best Of	$19.95
00694885 Spin Doctors – Pocket Full Of Kryptonite	$19.95
00120004 Steely Dan – Best Of	$24.95
00694921 Steppenwolf, The Best Of	$22.95
00694957 Rod Stewart – Unplugged...And Seated	$22.95
00690021 Sting – Fields Of Gold	$19.95
00694824 Best Of James Taylor	$16.95
00694887 Thin Lizzy – The Best Of Thin Lizzy	$19.95
00690022 Richard Thompson Guitar	$19.95
00690030 Toad The Wet Sprocket	$19.95
00694411 U2 – The Joshua Tree	$19.95
00690039 Steve Vai – Alien Love Secrets	$24.95
00690172 Steve Vai – Fire Garden	$22.95
00660137 Steve Vai – Passion & Warfare	$24.95
00694904 Vai – Sex and Religion	$24.95
00690023 Jimmie Vaughan – Strange Pleasures	$19.95
00690024 Stevie Ray Vaughan – Couldn't Stand The Weather	$19.95
00660136 Stevie Ray Vaughan – In Step	$19.95
00694879 Stevie Ray Vaughan – In The Beginning	$19.95
00690036 Stevie Ray Vaughan – Live Alive	$24.95
00694835 Stevie Ray Vaughan – The Sky Is Crying	$19.95
00690025 Stevie Ray Vaughan – Soul To Soul	$19.95
00690015 Stevie Ray Vaughan – Texas Flood	$19.95
00694776 Vaughan Brothers – Family Style	$19.95
00120026 Joe Walsh – Look What I Did...	$24.95
00694789 Muddy Waters – Deep Blues	$24.95
00690071 Weezer	$19.95